BHAGAVAD GITA

Dr Śrī Pundrik Goswami is a revered spiritual luminary and an inspiring voice of contemporary wisdom. He belongs to the exalted lineage of Śrī Gopal Bhatt Goswami—one of the six Goswamis personally initiated by Śrī Chaitanya Mahaprabhu and the founder of the sacred Śrī Radha Raman Temple in Vrindavan. Fondly known as Maharaj Ji, he stands as the 38th Āchārya of this divine tradition, initiated by his revered grandfather and Guru, Śrī Atul Krishna Goswami Ji Maharaj and lovingly nurtured by his father, Śrī Bhuti Krishna Goswami Ji Maharaj.

Endowed with a rare blend of scriptural depth and magnetic oratory, Maharaj Ji brings the timeless wisdom of the Vedas alive for the modern seeker. His discourses on Śrīmad Bhāgavatam, Śrī Rāma Kathā, Śrī Chaitanya Charitāmṛta, the Bhagavad Gītā and other sacred texts resonate across generations and cultures, touching hearts in India and around the world. In recognition of his profound contribution to spiritual and intellectual life, he has been conferred with a Doctorate (D.Litt.) by Mansarovar University, Bhopal (MP).

At the heart of his mission lies a deep commitment to the youth—guiding them to discover purpose, character and inner strength. Maharaj Ji regularly addresses students at educational institutions, professionals in multinational corporations and audiences at TED platforms, seminars and global forums, bridging ancient wisdom with contemporary challenges.

This vision is beautifully complemented by his wife, Renukā Goswami Ji, with whom he leads Nimai Pathshala, a sacred initiative dedicated to imparting scriptural knowledge and Vedic values free of cost to nearly 2,50,000 students, nurturing a generation rooted in culture, clarity and compassion.

Fluent in Hindi, English and Sanskrit, Maharaj Ji transcends barriers of age, nationality and background. His words do not merely inform, they transform, awakening devotion, discipline and direction in every listener.

Media handles:
Instagram: @sripundrik
Facebook: Acharya Sri Pundrik Goswami
YouTube: Sri Pundrik Goswami
Website: sripundrik.com

Interpreted by
Pundrik Goswami

BHAGAVAD GITA

Light of Divine Wisdom

Published by Westland Books, a division of Nasadiya Technologies Private Limited, in 2026

No. 269/2B, First Floor, 'Irai Arul', Vimalraj Street, Nethaji Nagar, Alapakkam Main Road, Maduravoyal, Chennai 600095

Westland and the Westland logo are the trademarks of Nasadiya Technologies Private Limited, or its affiliates.

Copyright © Pundrik Goswami, 2026

Pundrik Goswami asserts the moral right to be identified as the author of this work.

ISBN: 9789371977753

10 9 8 7 6 5 4 3 2 1

The views and opinions expressed in this work are the author's own and the facts are as reported by him, and the publisher is in no way liable for the same.

All rights reserved

Typeset by Jojy Philip
Printed at Parksons Graphics Pvt. Ltd

No part of this book may be reproduced, or stored in a retrieval system, or transmitted in any form or by any means, electronic, mechanical, photocopying, recording, or otherwise, without express written permission of the publisher.

Contents

Thoughts of Maharajshri — vii

Background — ix

1. Arjuna 'Vishaad' Yoga: Arjuna's Gloom — 1
2. Sankhya Yoga: The Yoga of Perfection — 10
3. Karma Yoga: The Yoga of Action — 21
4. Gyana Karma Sanyas Yoga: The Yoga of Renouncing Karma Through Knowledge — 32
5. Karma Sanyas Yoga: The Yoga of Renunciation of Action — 40
6. Dhyan Yoga: The Yoga of Meditation or Atma Sanyama Yoga — 48
7. Gyana Vigyan Yoga: Adhyatma Yoga — 59
8. Akshar Brahma Yoga: Tarak Brahma Yoga — 70
9. Raj Vidya Raj Guhya Yoga: The Yoga of Royal Knowledge and Royal Secret — 79
10. Vibhuti Yoga: The Yoga of Divine Manifestations — 89

11.	Vishwa Roopa Darshan Yoga: The Yoga of the Vision of the Universal Cosmic Form	100
12.	Bhakti Yoga: The Yoga of Devotion	111
13.	Kshetra Kshetragya Vibhaga Yoga: The Yoga of the Field and Knower of the Field	122
14.	Guna Traya Vibhaga Yoga: The Three Qualities of Material Nature	131
15.	Purushottam Yoga: The Yoga of the Divine	140
16.	Deva–Asura Sampad Vibhaga Yoga: The Yoga of Discerning the Divine and Demonic Endowments	150
17.	Shraddha Traya Vibhaga Yoga: The Yoga of the Division of Threefold Faith	158
18.	Moksha Sanyas Yoga: Liberation Through Renunciation	165

Thoughts of Maharajshri

One form of God is the 'Brahmanaad', the divine sound. Words become eternal when spoken from the depths of the atman, the soul. Shree Vyasa Deva transcribed the Vedas, which were transmitted orally in the past. He added Shree Krishna's divine and immortal words to the pantheon of spiritual texts. For eighteen days during the second Covid lockdown—16 April 2020 to 3 May 2020—I meditated on the eighteen chapters of the Bhagavad Gita, and I was blessed with a unique interpretation that has been written and presented here.

Pundrik Goswami

Background

In 2020, when the world was grappling with the devastation inflicted by the COVID-19 pandemic, people were forced to navigate an extremely challenging phase, both physically and mentally. However, even during the darkest hours faced by the world in this century, people were trying to alleviate others' suffering. Pondering on this global phenomenon, Maharaj Ji (Pundrik Goswami) was blessed with the insight to meditate. He made good use of this invaluable time at hand for the benefit of society. In his words, 'When one cannot go out, it is best to go within!'

The Pandava prince Arjuna was once crestfallen with despair, but Lord Krishna pulled him out of the abyss. Using this idea as his foundation, Maharaj Ji began his contemplations on the Gita, devoting one day to each chapter. He delved deep into the mysteries of each chapter and found pearls of wisdom. His is a unique, practical and simple analysis of this sacred text, which could help salvage ravaged and exhausted minds. His meditations took the form of this book, *Bhagavad Gita: Light of Divine Wisdom*.

1

Arjuna 'Vishaad' Yoga

Arjuna's Gloom
Total verses: 46

The first chapter of the Bhagavad Gita explains Arjuna's despondency, and to understand the text better, one must read the verses in succession. When a cow eats grass, she needs time to digest it. This process enables her to produce milk. Similarly, acharyas and sages ponder over the sacred texts before they can share their knowledge through sermons. I am sharing my observations here.

Sarvopanishado gaavo dogdha Gopalnandanah|
Partho vatsah sudhirbhokta dugdham Gitamritam mahatt||
(Gita Mahatmya 6)

(All the Upanishads are like a cow, and the one who milks the cow is Shree Krishna, the son of Nanda. Arjuna is the calf, the beautiful nectar of the Gita is the milk and fortunate devotees of fine intellect drink that milk.)

Before the battle of Mahabharata, Arjuna and the Kaurava prince Duryodhana went to Shree Krishna. It was the choice between the Almighty and His Maya (apparition). Blinded by the latter's glare, Duryodhana chose Shree Krishna's army. Arjuna, on the other hand, chose Shree Krishna, the primordial truth. It is the love for the truth that leads to satsang (holy company). Goswami Tulsidas, a saint in medieval India, wrote, '*Binu satsang bibek na hohi* (There is no conscience without satsang).' Our thoughts are shaped by the company we surround ourselves with.

We have all seen the picture of Shree Krishna and Arjuna sitting on a ratha (chariot). The chariot signifies the physical body or the material world. In this image, Shree Krishna represents our conscience, while Arjuna is the human mind. Many think that 'conscience' is synonymous with the mind, but a crucial difference separates the two concepts. The mind is the seat of one's conscience. We are all born with our minds, but the conscience develops gradually.

Shree Krishna and Arjuna on the Chariot

Many tend to skip the first chapter of the Bhagavad Gita. Perhaps it is because Shree Krishna does not speak in this portion; he only analyses the situation unfolding around him. As a result, readers do not want to explore the verses that are not ascribed to Krishna. This perspective is myopic. The Gita's first chapter is instrumental in teaching us how to gauge a situation before responding to it. We see how the mind attempts to instruct the conscience. Having been influenced by his mind, Arjuna is sucked into a maelstrom of delusion. To quote Maharaj Ji, 'The mind deludes, but your conscience can lead you to the truth.'

Shree Krishna brings Arjuna to the centre of the Kurukshetra battlefield. The Pandava prince stands at the crossroads of dharma (right) and adharma (wrong), but his mind deceives him, clouding his judgement into thinking of his enemies as his cousins, uncles and teachers. Caught in this snare of delusion, he cannot differentiate between truth and untruth. Arjuna's inner conflict becomes the foundation of this sacred text.

The Bhagavad Gita is a universal text. It possesses the power to uplift and develop humanity's conscience. It lends a spiritual dimension to the story of warring cousins. The war between the Pandavas and the Kauravas is a metaphor for the war between morality and immorality that rages inside each one of us. When the mind and conscience oppose each other, despair and gloom make room for themselves. The Gita is a gift that helps anchor and enrich the desolate mind.

When Arjuna considers his enemies as members of his family, he lays down his arms and refuses to fight. However, Shree Krishna urges him to fulfil his duty. When the pall of gloom finally dissipates, Shree Krishna asks him to fight without envy or jealousy.

There is a paradox at the heart of the Bhagavad Gita. For those who want to live like ascetics, Shree Krishna says encouragingly, 'I have created this beautiful world. Go and enjoy it!' Simultaneously, he cautions those who want to live a life of luxury: 'Beware!' he warns. 'The more you indulge in sensory pleasures, the more you get sucked into them.' Balancing these contradictory desires and forces is life's greatest goal. To comprehend and solve this paradox, Arjuna surrendered himself to Shree Krishna. Similarly, if we want to avoid drowning in a flood of conflicting thoughts, we, too, must surrender our minds to our vivek (conscience).

Our actions are controlled by either the mind or the conscience. The Gita's first chapter contrasts Arjuna's control with that of Shree Krishna's. By surrendering our minds to Shree Krishna, we allow wisdom to blossom. Whenever you find yourself faced with a choice, ask yourself: do I want to decide for myself or let Shree Krishna decide for me? To live a meaningful life, you must train your mind to serve you, not act against you. Through careful analysis, you can distinguish between the mind and conscience. The mind indulges in imagination, but your conscience is rooted in reality. The mind is clever and misleading; the conscience is steady and guides you towards righteousness. Although Arjuna is tempted to take the easy way out, Shree Krishna compels him to fight for dharma.

MIND	INTELLECT
Imagination	Reality
Tricks	Guidance
Distracts	Keeps focused
Misleads you	Leads you
Destruction	Construction
Weakens	Strengthens
Instant pleasure	Pain in the beginning
Sorrow in the end	Happiness in the end

The Chart of Mind and Intellect

The mind offers momentary pleasure, but the path it prescribes ends in misery. On the other hand, when we are attuned to our conscience, we might encounter pain in the beginning, but we will eventually find lasting happiness. If we had left our houses during the lockdown, we would have enjoyed a fleeting sense of freedom. Had we come into contact with an infected person, that joy would have quickly turned into misery. Staying indoors was the more difficult option, but practising restraint guaranteed safety. Your conscience is the fog light that illuminates the path ahead as you drive through a blanket of haze on a dark night. Your mind, however, will only lead you to a dead end.

The first chapter sets the stage for a dialogue between Shree Krishna and Arjuna, that is, between the conscience and the mind. 'Vivek' is innate in every individual. *Ayogya purosho nasti yojakastatra durlabhaha* (No person is unworthy, but scarce is the enabler) (Subhashita). The smoker is aware that smoking is injurious to his health. Gory warnings are displayed on the packet of cigarettes he carries everywhere. Even then, each time he lights a cigarette, the mind triumphs over the conscience. An alcoholic wakes up nearly every morning with a throbbing headache. Well-versed with the adverse effects of drinking, he vows never to touch the bottle again. Yet, as evening approaches, he starts thinking of alcohol again. This demonstrates how one's mind tries to overpower one's conscience, forcing one into doing something wrong. This process is explained in the Gita's first chapter.

When gripped by dejection, we must turn inwards and listen to our conscience. A strengthened conscience guides us prudently. A weak conscience is easily subjugated by the mind into making wrong decisions. If you want to become physically strong, you exercise and follow a healthy diet. To fortify the intellect, you must rely on satsang for positive energy. Many people find it hard to give up bad habits, but the moment they come in contact with a divine or noble personality, they feel empowered to give up those habits instantly.

This is the power of good company. When in the company of sages and ascetics, the most materialistic people become saintly. Through satsang, enquiry, positive thinking and meditation, we can expand the intellect.

A positive mindset is especially important in today's world, where the majority live their lives like the blind Dhritarashtra, the Kaurava king who was unable or unwilling to see the truth. For example, people wear uncomfortable clothes simply because it's fashionable. Fashion constantly changes—from loose to tight, long to short—and people follow these trends blindly. Many claim they are not habitual drinkers, yet give in to the vice because of the company they keep. Why fall into such traps? To rise above them, one needs to empower the intellect and reach a higher level. This enhancement is achieved through good company and positive thinking. The difference between the conscience and the mind is that the former is open to reason, while the latter is not.

Dhritarashtra was born blind, but Gandhari, his wife, decided to blindfold herself. A blind mind and a *blinded* conscience gave birth to the demons that threatened to annihilate the world. To witness the battle of Kurukshetra, Dhritarashtra had to rely on Sanjaya's narration, a cautious and far-sighted individual. Veda Vyasa had blessed Sanjaya with the power of intuition that enabled him to see far into the distance. Utilising his sharp vision, he helped a blind Dhritarashtra watch the events of the Mahabharata unfold. Like Sanjaya, a guru sees and shows. Learn only from such a person.

Dhritarashtra once questions Sanjaya:

> *Dharmakshetrey Kurukshetrey samaveta yuyutsavaha|*
> *Maamakaha Paandavashchaiva kimkurvata Sanjaya||*
> (Gita 1:1)

(O Sanjaya! After gathering on the holy field of Kurukshetra, what did my sons and the sons of Pandu, being so desirous to fight, do?)

Pay close attention to the first two words of the shloka (verse). 'Sow the field of "karma" with the seeds of "dharma"!' If you sow the seeds of unrighteousness, you will only spread anarchy. But if they are seeds of righteousness, you shall reap the fruit of bliss. Shree Krishna remains maun (quiet) throughout the first chapter. In the opening verses, a blind man asks questions of Sanjaya, revealing the former's lack of awareness. Arjuna, by contrast, is aware of his ignorance. Herein lies the fundamental difference between Dhritarashtra and Arjuna. If you want to understand the Gita in eighteen days, you must begin by understanding your situation. Set aside your arguments and read carefully. Only then will you experience the beauty of this wonderful text.

A frightened Duryodhana tells Bheeshma and Dronacharya,

Aparyapttam tadasmaakam balam Bheeshmarakshittam|
Parayapttam twidmeytesham balam Bheemabhirakshittam||
(Gita 1:10)

(Our strength is immeasurable, and we are protected by Grandfather Bheeshma, whereas the strength of the Pandavas, protected by Bhima, is limited.)

Duryodhana tries to camouflage his fear with guile because his ego controls his senses. Arjuna, too, is scared. Even then, he surrenders to Shree Krishna. This highlights the difference in their upbringing. Between verses twenty and twenty-five, Arjuna is ready to fight. From verses twenty-six to thirty, when he surveys the battlefield and sees the elders whom he deeply respects standing in opposition, he begins to question his future actions. In verses thirty-one to thirty-seven, he is arguing with Jagadeesh (the Almighty), putting forth flimsy arguments—the world will come to an end, how will he face himself and so on. From verses thirty-eight to forty-seven, Arjuna is completely overwhelmed with grief. He casts aside his weapons.

Our physical body, which is represented by Arjuna's chariot, is the driving force of the soul. As has been stated before, the dialogue between Arjuna and Shree Krishna is a conversation between the soul and the conscience, between the atman and paramatman. The mind has overpowered the conscience and commands it to be taken to the midst of the battlefield. Drowning in a flood of emotions, it is unable to perceive the truth. In the next chapter, Shree Krishna will begin his sermon through Sankhya Yoga, the path of proper deliberation, calculation and enumeration. Arjuna is saved because he chose Shree Krishna, meaning the mind chose prudence and discretion. Shree Krishna, the sadguru, begins instructing his disciple, Partha. After being reprimanded by the conscience in the second chapter, the mind surrenders. Unless the conscience is empowered, one cannot overcome grief. In truth, this grief is a form of prasad (blessing). Let our grief lead us to God!

Only when your lead thoughts are pure and holy will your mind be healthy. If you desire a healthy mind, rein it in with the support of your conscience.

SUMMARY

Verses 1–2:	Introduction
Verses 3–11:	Duryodhana's deliverance
Verses 12–19:	The tumultuous sound of the conch shells
Verses 20–25:	Arjuna is ready for battle
Verses 26–30:	Arjuna is plagued with emotions
Verses 31–37:	Arjuna's arguments
Verses 38–47:	Arjuna's collapse

KEY QUOTES

1. The company of truth is satsang, and the 'prasad' is vivek.
2. The mind takes you towards moha (attachment), while vivek leads you to truth.
3. The mind cannot discriminate between truth and untruth.
4. The greatest gift of the Gita is that it empowers your mind.
5. The more you have, the less you will be able to enjoy it.
6. Plough the field of karma with dharma.
7. A guru is that far-sighted person who can both see and make you see.
8. Are you a guide? Can you lead?
9. When your thoughts are pure and holy, the mind will be healthy.

2

Sankhya Yoga

The Yoga of Perfection
Total verses: 72

The second chapter of the Bhagavad Gita, Sankhya Yoga, is based on the core teachings of this divine text. It is the knowledge of the self. Bade Maharaj Shree Atul Krishna Goswami Maharaj would say, 'It is a topic of serious contemplation. Arjuna is listening to Shree Krishna's exhortation with rapt attention.' We need to devote some time to this, and I am confident that this study will elevate our consciousness.

I say, '*Appa Deepo Bhava* (Be your light).' Arjuna's devotion and dedication enabled him to gain the insight that led him to choose Shree Krishna. Arjuna symbolises the mind! He chooses Shree Krishna, that is, truth, '*Saancho ek Radharaman, jhutho sab sansar* (Only Shree Radha Raman is real and the world is illusory).' When Shree Krishna and Arjuna are seated on the chariot, the conscience and the mind are together. When the mind commands the conscience to reach the middle of the battlefield, the result is distress. Shree Krishna remains silent in the first chapter. Intelligence often leads to arguments, but it is discrimination that reasons. Shree Vasudev Ji carries baby Krishna to Gokul in a basket; the act symbolises wisdom. This wisdom grants us the power to differentiate between right and wrong, thereby revealing the ultimate reality. A tiny firefly can show the way in utter darkness! The world is an amazing amalgamation of nature and the divine. Though nature replenishes itself, today its exploitation has crossed all limits. Wars, pain and suffering plague humanity. Shrimad Bhagavatam observes that humans, being a superior species, can enjoy the beauty of the world, but Shree Krishna says: '*Mam upetya punar janma duḥkhaalayam ashaasvatam* (Attaining me, you don't need to be born in this transient world full of miseries)' (Gita 8:15). It is said, '*Agyan timirandhasya gyanananjan shalakaya, Agyan is timir,* (Ignorance is darkness)', and guru = gu (darkness) + ru (light). The one who shows the light is the guru. Jagatguru Shree Krishna says that the world is indeed full of sorrow. But if the lamp of wisdom is kindled through the guru's grace, one finds the clarity to see rightly and act with true discretion! Arjuna is completely shattered. Lord Krishna says, 'O Arjuna! There is nothing to grieve, arise and awake!' These words are not meant for Arjuna alone; through him, Shree Krishna addresses all of humanity.

Today, the highest-selling medicine in the world is antidepressants. As depression assumes pandemic proportions, the cure lies in the Gita. Our elders would always tell us to stay healthy, and be content and happy. A person immersed in pure love is always blissful. The problem is that neither are we happy nor do we want others to enjoy happiness. If anything, it makes us jealous. Arjuna became embroiled in all sorts of delusions on the battlefield of his own volition. Usually, when we are sad, even a small gesture of sympathy from someone can bring us a sense of relief. But Shree Krishna does not do so. Instead, he reprimands Arjuna and says;

> *Klaibyaṁ maa sma gamaḥ Partha naitattvayya upapadyate|*
> *Kṣhuddram hṛdaya-daurballyaṁ tyaktvottiṣṭha parantapa||*
> (Gita 2:3)

(O Partha! This unmanly behaviour does not befit you. Give up this weakness and arise, O vanquisher of enemies.)

'How did this impotence creep into you? How did you become so weak?' No one has ever called Arjuna impotent, but Lord Krishna admonishes him. Parth (the son of Pritha or Kunti) is an archer extraordinaire. This conversation happens on the battlefield. We, too, are constantly at war, whether internal or external. To win this war, we first need to understand the nature of the world. In the second chapter of the Bhagavad Gita, three key points are highlighted:

I. THE TRUE NATURE OF THE WORLD

According to our scriptures, there are two faces of the world:

a) The World Is Perpetually in a State of Duality

Duality is inherent in the world; in other words, it is either this or that! The Manas (Ramcharitmanas) says, '*Haani laabh jeevan maran, yash apayash Bidhi haath* (Loss or gain, life or death, fame or infamy, are in the hands of God).' The Gita says:

> *Samaḥ shatrau cha mitre cha tatha maanapamaanayoho|*
> *Sheetoṣhṇa-sukhaduḥkheṣu samaḥ sanga-vivarjitaha||*
> (Gita 12:18)

(Treat both friend or foe respectfully, equipoised in honour or dishonour, bearing cold or heat and joy or sorrow, beware of bad company.)

On the material level comes profit or loss. At the physical level, we encounter pleasure and pain. On the mental or emotional level, feelings of happiness and sorrow arise. On the intellectual level, we deal with respect and disrespect. These dualities perpetually exist in the world. At first, one is bothered about profit or loss at the material level. Then, as consciousness shifts, the focus moves on to the physical level where survival and bodily well-being take precedence. In the face of any calamity, one tries to save oneself. The movement of our consciousness is inwards—from the gross to the micro. On the mental plane, material and physical concerns begin to fade. The emotional quotient takes centre stage. But as we transcend emotional turbulence, consciousness enters the intellectual domain. Consider Stephen Hawking. He surpassed material, physical and emotional barriers to explore the vastness of the universe for the benefit of mankind. Another inspiring example is the Brooklyn Bridge in New York. When the idea of constructing the bridge was first proposed, most engineers of the time outrightly rejected it. Only John Roebling took it upon himself to go ahead with the plan. Several minor and major accidents derailed their plans. In one such incident, many people died, and Roebling was seriously injured and was paralysed. At that time, the bridge was only two-thirds complete, and the other engineers were not well-versed with the plan. Though bedridden and unable to speak or move, Roebling could still move one finger. Using a single finger, he began communicating with his wife and instructed her on how to execute the rest of the plan. Overcoming all odds, the bridge was completed in fourteen years. Some even call it the eighth wonder of the World. Ultimately, after crossing the material, physical and emotional plane, the consciousness reaches the spiritual level, devoid of all dualities.

b) The World Is Ever-changing

The world is always in a state of flux. It is filled with surprises, but such unexpected changes don't necessarily excite us because we haven't anticipated or evaluated them. When unforeseen shifts occur in the world, we become distressed.

Therefore, we must accept the world as it is, rather than what we expect it to be. Acceptance is bliss. Gurus don't seek to change the world; they help us understand it. Understanding leads to detachment. Those who tried to change the world according to their expectations, like Mussolini and Hitler, unleashed anarchy. Similarly, man's disregard for nature has resulted in climate crisis. The problem is that we expect others to change, but we don't change ourselves.

Accepting people as they are leads to inner peace. The Buddha remained unaffected by insults hurled at him because he was operating from a higher spiritual plane and was able to ignore them. He taught us to evaluate, understand and accept before responding to any situation.

True transformation begins with us. We must learn to change ourselves instead of striving to change the world. The mind's duality turns love into hatred! The Gita emphasises acceptance, and this chapter describes the true nature of the world.

Examine the world carefully.
Assess it.
Understand it.
Accept it.
And enjoy it.

There are four levels of existence: the soul, the intellect, the mind and the body. Each experience has different dualities. At the gross level, we feel loss or gain. Physically, we experience joy or sorrow. Emotionally, we encounter victory or defeat. Intellectually, it is about respect or insult. Finally, surpassing all, the spiritual level is anand (pure bliss).

Vasaaṃsi jeerṇaani yatha vihaaya navani gṛhuṇaati naroparaaṇi|
Tathaa shareeraṇi vihaaya jeerṇaan anyani saṃyati navaani dehi||
(Gita 2:22)

(Just as a person sheds worn-out garments and wears new ones,
the soul discards old bodies and takes on new ones.)

This beautiful verse has always stayed with me. When my father passed away, it gave me immense strength. I found solace within myself through the words of God. At the spiritual level, let us examine who we are. By transcending the macro and micro levels of existence, we come to realise that we are not merely the body but also the soul—an eternal part of the Supreme Being.

Nainaṃ chindanti shastraaṇi nainaṃ dahati paavakaha|
Na chainaṃ kledayantyapo na shoṣhayati marutaha||
(Gita 2:23)

(Weapons cannot hurt it, fire cannot burn it, water cannot wet it
and wind cannot dry it.)

We evolve across the material, physical, mental, intellectual and spiritual levels. In reality, we give up nothing; we simply elevate ourselves. Renunciation doesn't mean giving up; it means rising above. We hesitate to grow because we are scared. However, the only way forward is through practice and detachment; '*Abhyaasena tu Kaunteya vairaagyena cha gṛhuyate* (By practice and detachment, one can achieve mastery, O Arjuna)' (Gita 6:35).

So, the question is, where are we? By expanding our consciousness, we become the spectator and see.

The Dalai Lama says, 'We sacrifice our health to earn wealth and then sacrifice wealth to regain health.' Shree Shankaracharya says, '*Ekaanttey sukhamaasyatam*'—practise quietude to experience bliss. Shree Raghunath Das Goswami has practised this, and he says, '*Manaḥ shikṣha* (Teach your mind).' Indeed, this proves that we are not the mind.

A monk embraces solitude by limiting his worldly interactions and increasing his spiritual practice. This is renunciation. When we reach the fifth stage of evolution, the world ceases to affect us. While the body, mind and intellect are attracted to worldly pleasures, the soul remains unaffected. It functions as our spectator. When one dies, the external world, body, mind and intellect remain here. The soul separates, carrying forward the subtle impressions of past births.

II. THE NATURE OF THE SOUL

We must address the question, 'Who am I?' Shree Krishna says, '*Vasaamsi jeernaani yatha vihaaya navani grhunati naro'parani* (Just as a person discards worn-out garments and puts on new ones, the soul casts off its worn-out bodies and takes on new ones).'

Let us understand this stage by stage, as it defines our very existence. The body comes first, then the mind, followed by the intellect and, finally, our guiding force, the soul.

The most important question we must ask ourselves is, where is our consciousness focused? Spirituality cannot be truly experienced by the body, nor through the mind or even the intellect. It is the domain of the soul alone. The soul is a divine gift, eternal and unchanging. The Gita explains our nature and identity.

III. THE ABILITY TO INTERACT WITH THE WORLD

The world is a subject of experience, and we are here to experience its wonders. It is an object of enjoyment, and we are the ones who must learn to enjoy it. Without understanding this, how can one interact effectively? Two verses are particularly beneficial while understanding the propriety of our experiences and interactions:

> *Kutastva kashmalamidam vishamey samupasthitam|*
> *Anaaryajushtama svargyama keertikaram Arjuna||*
> (Gita 2:2)

(The Supreme Lord says, O Arjuna! How come this delusion has overcome you in this hour of peril? It does not befit you. Instead of the heavenly abode, it pulls you down, disgraced.)

Klaibyaṁ maa sma gamaḥ Partha naitattvayyupapadyate|
Kṣhuddraṁ hridayadaurballyaṁ tyaktvottiṣṭha Parantapa||
(Gita 2:3)

(O Partha! Do not yield to such impotence. Cast off this wretched weakness and arise, O scorcher of enemies.)

Till the tenth shloka, Arjuna is yet to emerge from his profound grief. From verses 11 to 25, Lord Krishna begins revealing the nature of the immortal atman.

Maatrasparshastu Kaunteya sheetoṣhṇa sukhaduḥkhadaḥa|
Aagamaapayino anitya staṁstitikṣhasva Bharata||
(Gita 2:14)

(O son of Kunti! The contact between the senses and the sense objects gives rise to fleeting perceptions of happiness and distress. They are transitory, like the summer and winter months. O descendant of Bharat! Learn to tolerate them.)

From verse 26 to 30, Lord Krishna instructs him not to grieve. From 31 to 38, he elaborates on the duties of a Kshatriya. From 39 to 53, he describes Nishkama (Unselfish) Karma Yoga.

Vyavasaayatmika buddhir ekeha Kurunandana|
Bahushaakha hyanantashcha buddhayo avyavasaayinam||
(Gita 2:41)

(O descendant of the Kurus! The intellect of those treading this path is resolute and single-pointed. But the irresolute are shaky.)

From verse 53 to 72, Shree Krishna talks about the state of a Sthit Pragya (calm, content and free from desires).

Sthitapragyasya kaa bhaṣa samaadhisthasya Keshava|
Sthitadhihi kiṁ prabhaṣeta kimaseet vrajeta kim||
(Gita 2:54)

(Arjuna asks, O Keshava! What is the disposition of the one who experiences Samadhi? How does an enlightened person sit, walk and talk?)

Now, Arjuna sees the light of day. He moves upwards and enquires about the higher states. Lord Krishna says:

Prajahaati yada kaaman sarvan Partha manogataan|
Aatmanyevaatmana tuṣhṭaḥ sthitaprgyastadochyate||
(Gita 2:55)

(O Partha! When one gives up all desire of sense gratification, which arise from an inebriated mind, and the mind thus purified abides in the self and a state of transcendental consciousness.)

Therefore, the three most important characteristics are:
1. Being stable, whether experiencing pain or in joy.
2. Being in control of the mind and the senses.
3. Being free from the dualities of the world.

This is the essence of Sankhya Yoga, described elaborately in the third canto of the Shrimad Bhagavatam. It essentially involves the understanding of the twenty-four elements or the evolution of nature.

There is an atheistic interpretation of the Sankhya philosophy that excludes the twenty-fifth element and regards nature as the ultimate supreme. However, Lord Kapila (an avatar of Vishnu) revealed the theistic Sankhya to Mata Devahuti (his mother), introducing the twenty-fifth element, the Paramatman Tattva, the Supreme Personality of Godhead. The twenty-four elements alone cannot create the universe. It is only in the presence of the twenty-fifth, the Divine, that creation becomes possible. Today, even science is talking about the God Particle.

Sankhya Yoga Components	Elements
Five great elements (Pancha Mahabhutas)	Earth, water, fire, air, ether
Five organs of action (Pancha Karma Indriyas)	Hands, feet, mouth, organ of excretion, genitals
Five sense organs (Pancha Gyana Indriyas)	Eyes, nose, ears, tongue, skin
Five subtle elements (Pancha Tan-matras)	Sound, touch, form, taste, smell
Additional four elements	Mind (manas), intellect (buddhi), consciousness (chitta), ego (ahamkara)

Sankhya is the root of science. The definitions of vigyan (science) and gyana (knowledge) are distinct. They are two different aspects, but the confusion arises when science is equated with knowledge.

Until this is understood, it will be difficult to find peace. We should read it carefully; if we don't understand, read it again. Now, let us enlighten ourselves with this divine light! Satsang is not only a necessity but also is a curative therapy.

SUMMARY

Verse 1:	Sanjaya presents the introductory aspect.
Verses 2–3:	The influence of the previous chapter on Arjuna.
Verses 4–10:	Arjuna expresses his sorrow.
Verses 11–25:	Krishna introduces the concept of the eternal soul.
Verses 26–30:	Krishna motivates Arjuna not to grieve.
Verses 31–38:	Krishna explains duty.

Verses 39–53: Krishna elaborates on Nishkama Karma Yoga (selfless action).

Verses 53–72: Krishna describes the characteristics of a wise man (Sthit Pragya).

KEY QUOTES

1. The Gita provides us with a deep perspective to understand ourselves, the tools to know the world and the ability to interact with it.
2. The world must serve the mahatma, and it is imperative that the mahatma takes care of our minds.
3. Accept the world as it is, not as you want it to be.
4. Gurus do not change the world; they help us understand it.
5. Light the lamp of knowledge.
6. Renunciation does not mean giving up; it is a process of elevation.
7. First, evaluate the world, then understand it, accept it and enjoy it.

3

Karma Yoga

The Yoga of Action
Total verses: 43

The values of Sanatan Dharma are ingrained in the Indian psyche, nurturing wisdom and inner balance. With proper guidance, people come to understand these timeless principles and act accordingly.

Gita is the song of Lord Krishna. Among the different texts, about 350 are available today, such as the Ashtavakra Gita, Uddhava Gita, Rama Gita, Guru Gita, etc. But amongst this vast corpus, the Bhagavad Gita stands out.

The Bhagavad Gita is a divine gift from Shree Krishna to the jeeva (man), and the Gopi Geet, the song of love sung by the gopis (the maidens of Vrindavan), is the jeeva's expression of divine love.

As Maharaj Ji puts it, 'The Supreme Personality of Godhead revealed the ultimate truth to the world, and his lovers expressed their love for the Supreme.' According to Shrimad Bhagavatam, Arjuna and the gopis of Vrindavan met at Kurukshetra, which became the Dharma Kshetra because they shared their divine experiences there. 'Kurukshetra' signifies the field of action ('Kuru' means 'to do'). The third chapter, Karma Yoga, is all about action. Understanding the Gita requires concentration because it is a serious dialogue between the jeeva (man) and the paramatman (Divine). A thorough understanding is necessary to experience its divinity.

Before we proceed further, let us revisit the core aspects of the second chapter. It talks about four key points and defines the twenty-five elements of Sankhya Yoga. When these twenty-five elements coalesced to create the universe, the Divine emerged from the cosmic egg as Narayana: '*Narayaṇa viraajitaḥ yasya saha Narayaṇaḥ.*'

Narayana, the four-armed form of Lord Krishna, the Lord of Vaikuntha, appeared holding a conch, discus, mace and a lotus, each symbolising the four dimensions of our existence.

The lotus, also known as a pundarik, signifies purity and beauty. It blooms above the mud and represents the spiritual aspect of the soul. Divine beauty is often described as the lotus. Interestingly, the lotus is not a creation of Brahma (the Creator). He emerges from the lotus, signifying spiritual evolution.

The conch stands for intellect and wisdom. In the Gita, Lord Krishna sounded his panchajanya (conch), symbolising the awakening of intellect through the Brahmanaad, the divine inner sound.

The third symbol, the discus, is the mind, manaschakrey. In yogic practices, we pass through the seven energy centres or chakras of the astral body. The sacral, or the Svadhisthana Chakra, is denoted by the Sudarshan Chakra. Transcending these seven chakras through meditation leads to mastery over the mind. Lastly, the mace represents our physical existence. The four-faced Lord Brahma appears through Narayana's navel. The four faces are: dharma (righteousness), artha (wealth), kama (desire) and moksha (liberation), respectively, known as the Chatur Purushartha (objects of human pursuit).

	Attributes	Purusharthas	Components
1	Conch	Dharma	Intellect
2	Mace	Artha	Body
3	Discus	Kama	Mind
4	Lotus	Moksha	Soul

Artha refers to material prosperity and is depicted by the mace, indicating strength and power. Kama is connected to the mind and is symbolised by the discus, representing the mind's inclination towards seeking pleasure and desire. Dharma, illustrating moral and ethical conduct, is connected to the intellect and typified by the conch, which stands for righteousness and the call of duty. Finally, moksha, or liberation, is linked to the soul and is embodied in the lotus, representing purity, detachment and rising above worldly existence.

Together, these four goals—dharma, artha, kama and moksha—are the Chatur Purushartha, as described in the scriptures. Shree Chaitanya Mahaprabhu interprets moksha as total detachment of the self from the world:

Dvi pade vandh mokṣhasya satyam satyam vadaamyaham|
Mameti baadhyate jantu na mameti vimuchyate||

(This shloka emphasises the concepts of attachment and detachment as the cause of bondage and liberation.)

There is a fifth Purushartha, the Prema Tattva, or divine love.

The Bhagavad Gita is not an ordinary historical narrative; it is the eternal manual of life, bestowed upon us by the Divine. You must have heard of Lego, a popular building toy for all age groups. Along with thousands of small pieces, you receive a reference picture and a manual. Similarly, we have been gifted this invaluable human birth, like a Lego set, but we seem to have misplaced the guiding document. This universal manual has been rediscovered by our gurus. Despite war, strife, pain, sorrow, murders, atrocities, etc., casting dark shadows of gloom on humanity, there are fleeting moments of joy. These instances are as ephemeral as a water bubble, visible one moment and gone the next. Our expectations become the cause of our pain. '*Mamupetya punarjanma duḥkhaalayamashaasvatam* (After attaining me, the realised souls do not return to this transitory world, full of miseries)' (Gita 8:15). Detachment from the world is the source of bliss. The joy we experience is not the same as that experienced by divine souls like Meera, Narsi, Nanak, Tukaram and Jana Bai. Can we revel in bliss all the time? They, too, are humans, but their lives inspire us. *Ayogyaḥ puruṣho naasti yojakastatra durlabhaḥ* (An ineligible person doesn't get it, for the right opportunity doesn't come easy) (Subhashita).

To learn, we need the Gita's guidance, as taught by Jagatguru Shree Krishna. By imbuing morality in our lives, we move from merely *existing* to truly *living*. Let me add that simply reading, worshipping or memorising a few shlokas is not enough; we need to understand them and live by them.

Gyana Yoga concerns the intellect, Bhakti Yoga is about the heart and Karma Yoga, where we are now, concerns the body. Arjuna is goaded to wake up from his deep slumber of ignorance by casting off all the inhibitions, being receptive and practising this yoga.

So, what does the Bhagavad Gita do?

- It is the eternal manual for life.
- It acts as a handbook of remedies to deal with disturbances, pressures, depression, conflicts and anxiety.
- It transforms our existence.
- It provides precise guidelines for action.
- It imparts knowledge about pure devotion.
- It explains why we do what we do and the source of those actions.

The Gita talks about pure love-infused devotion, which enables clarity of thought. Without clarity on what and how to do, one cannot attain perfection.

Why do we perform actions? The primary reasons are:

1. Compulsion: Many individuals act out of compulsion or claim to be compelled by circumstances. No circumstance can compel anyone. If one feels compelled, then they are yet to understand the science of karma. No one can compel us because we are free from external forces. However, we are not free from ourselves. Lethargy is compelling, and, in such cases, there is no genuine motivation; any effort becomes then superficial.
2. Wealth: Money is not the goal; it is just a platform. If the objective is only money, then being engaged in any activity is not a meaningful pursuit; it is just a waste of time and energy.
3. Passion: Are we passionate about work, going beyond money and compulsion? Are we enthusiastic about it? Passion drives one to work without being solely driven by financial gain. Those who are passionate work despite adversity.
4. Joy: Do we find joy in our work? If one is passionate, one enjoys working and is happy.

5. Happiness: Joy is followed by happiness, which signifies fulfilment. So, we must enjoy what we are doing.
6. Philanthropy: Do we work for the benefit of others? *'Parahita saris dharam nahi bhai, Paropakaaraya phalanti vrikshaha'* (There is no virtue greater than serving others; trees bear fruit for the benefit of others). The virtues of charity have been recognised and upheld through the ages. When we engage in philanthropy, all other qualities follow. We act out of happiness, not compulsion, because philanthropy is a fulfilling practice.
7. Spiritual awakening: Spiritual awakening follows a philanthropic spirit. Have we ever tried to work towards our spiritual upliftment? Sitting quietly by the Ganges, Parikshit Maharaj (Arjuna's grandson) heard the Shrimad Bhagavatam to attain liberation or moksha. He listened intently. He asked Srila Shukadeva, 'What is the duty of a dying man?' He was seeking spiritual nourishment.
8. Enlightenment: The eighth stage is self-enlightenment and imparting spiritual knowledge for the development of humanity. When we speak, our ears listen, and when our heart speaks, the heart listens. When the soul speaks, the soul listens, and when God speaks, God listens. This is the profound truth.

Japanese psychologist Michiko Kumano said that ikigai is a state of well-being that arises from devotion to activities one enjoys—activities that also bring a sense of fulfilment. Therefore, we need to focus on purpose, not profit. Mahatma Gandhi said, 'Have purpose in life and the means will follow!' It is important to reflect on whether one is working out of desire or necessity. Work has the potential to either purify or pollute us, bring peace or stress, liberate or imprison us. Understanding the source of our actions is crucial.

The Gita teaches us the art of living by transforming our mere existence into a life of purpose and fulfilment. By applying its principles, we can better navigate the complexities of life. So, what is kamya karma, or actions driven by desire? Imagine a man sweeping outside Shree Radha Raman's temple. At that moment, there could be two sentiments running through his mind: 'I am sweeping so that Shree Radha Raman Ji will give me wealth.' Or, 'Today, I have received the fruits of my past lives, as I have been granted the privilege of sweeping these hallowed precincts.' The first sentiment is kamya karma; the second sees the action as an opportunity.

Now, let us focus on the source of our actions. What is the driving force behind the things we do?

- Profit or loss?
- Desire-driven or obligatory?
- Forced or conscientious?
- Stressful or peaceful?
- Polluting or purifying?
- Binding or liberating?

If actions are limited to the body, they remain routine tasks, such as waking up early, going to work, driving a vehicle, etc. However, when one is driven by emotion, the mind becomes the source of action, indicating emotional and mental attachment. I have observed many instances where, when emotions are involved, the work itself becomes a source of joy. For example, a woman may clean her house as a routine. But when a sadhu praises her, saying, 'Ma! Your house feels like a temple with Lord Radha Raman residing here,' she feels emotionally charged. Then, she no longer sees herself as simply cleaning her house but serving a temple.

Actions originating from the subtle mind and intellect awaken our consciousness. The different sources of our actions and their nature are as follows:

If the source is the body, it is routine.
If the source is the mind, it is exciting.

If the source is the intellect, it is a matter of faith.
If the source is the subtle body, it awakens the consciousness.

There are three types of actions:
1. Obligatory,
2. Desire-driven and
3. Forbidden.

Each corresponds to a different nature: rajasic (passionate), sattvic (pure) and tamasic (ignorant). What is rejected by our consciousness is forbidden. Our wants shape our desire-driven actions, while the obligatory actions form a part of our duty.

In this chapter, Shree Krishna explains how to make karma (our actions) a form of yagya (sacrifice). Yagya is offering. We say 'swaha' while offering our ablutions, meaning self-surrender or offering with humility. Actions performed out of compulsion, for monetary gain, passion, pleasure or happiness, cannot be considered a sacrifice. These are superficial, constantly changing and rooted in duality. An action becomes yagya or worship only when it is performed with the sole purpose of spiritual growth.

At the start, Arjuna is confused. He questions why Lord Krishna is urging him to engage in such a dreadful act. He sees his revered teacher Dronacharya, grand sire Bheeshma and members of his kin standing before him, ready to fight. He is conflicted: should he fight the elders for the sake of the kingdom? Lord Krishna explains that great personalities, though aware of the outcome, still choose to fight because of a strong sense of duty.

Here, Arjuna is focused on his happiness and gain. Shree Krishna teaches that one should not act for material rewards, but for spiritual awakening. Duty, when performed as an act of worship, becomes 'Karma Yoga'. In verses 3 to 19, the Lord Krishna logically explains the nature of karma, describing it as an act of sacrifice. However, seeing Arjuna crestfallen, Lord Krishna encourages and motivates him into action, in verses 20 to 24.

Karmannaiva hi samsiddhim asthita janakaadayah|
Loka-sangraham evaapi sampashyan kartumarhasi||
(Gita 3:20)

(By performing actions alone, King Janaka and others attained perfection. You should also perform your duty as exempli gratia, maintaining the world order.)

Whatever a great person does, society follows. From verses 25 to 35, the technique of karma is explained with an analytical description. In these verses, Lord Krishna elucidates the nature of selfless action.

Mayi sarvaani karmaani samnyasyadhyatmachetasaha|
Nirashirnirsamo bhutva yudhyasva vigatajvaraha||
(Gita 3:30)

(Renouncing all actions in Me, with the mind focused on the self, free from hope and possessiveness and mental sickness, engage in battle.)

The methodology is explained up to the 35th verse.

Sreyansvadharmo vigunaah paradharmaatsvanushthitaat|
Svadharmey nidhanam shreyaha paradharmo bhayaavahah||
(Gita 3:35)

(It is better to perform one's duty imperfectly than to perform another's duty perfectly. Death in the course of performing one's duty is better than performing the duties of others, which is fraught with danger.)

In the 36th verse, Arjuna shows a spark of enthusiasm. Even then, the mental constrictions persist. He is a person who knows what to do but is unable to do it. The obstacles one encounters while performing righteous actions are explained by Lord Krishna in verses 37 to 39.

Kama esha krodha esha rajogunasamudbhavaha|
Mahashano mahapaapma viddhyenamih vairinaam||
(Gita 3:37)

(Desire and anger, born of passion, are insatiable and sinful. Know them as powerful adversaries in the world.)

From verses 40 to 43, Lord Krishna explains a comprehensive method to eliminate the barriers and obstacles to spiritual growth. This chapter, Karma Yoga, offers a profound understanding of action. Action is not merely a physical activity; rather, it is the intention behind the action that determines whether it is righteous or not. For example, both a doctor and a murderer may hold the knife and cut through flesh. However, the doctor's cut saves a life, while the murderer kills. The intention defines our action. All actions must lead to devotion. Pure love awakens wisdom.

Take this lamp, and let its flame enlighten the path. This lamp will help us find the way home. Reflecting on this, let's elevate our actions to the level of a sacred offering at the Divine Lotus Feet!

SUMMARY

Verses 1–2:	Arjuna faces a dilemma about being urged to perform forbidden actions.
Verses 3–19:	Krishna shares logical arguments about action.
Verses 20–24:	Krishna motivates Arjuna.
Verses 25–35:	Krishna explains the technique of action.
Verse 36:	Arjuna is enthused, but his inner conflict remains.
Verses 37–39:	Krishna describes the obstacles to righteous action.
Verses 40–43:	Krishna details the process to remove these obstacles.

KEY QUOTES

1. Unwholesome thoughts can only be conquered by wholesome thoughts.
2. Action is not just an activity; the intention behind it fulfils it.
3. Pure love awakens understanding, making our actions righteous.
4. Right action performed for the good of mankind becomes yagya.
5. Reflect on whether your actions purify or pollute.

4

Gyana Karma Sanyas Yoga

The Yoga of Renouncing Karma Through Knowledge

Total verses: 43

The study of any scripture becomes truly possible only under the guidance of an experienced teacher. Unless one turns inwards, a spiritual aspirant cannot begin to fathom divine wisdom. The Gita is a spiritual compass, guiding us through life's journey by uplifting our spirits and sharpening our intellect. Simply reading the text is exhilarating, but to understand and internalise its teachings, we need to study it very carefully. Dhritarashtra, for example, heard its message, but he couldn't grasp it because his mind was wandering.

No one has ever fully mastered this profound text. Great acharyas and spiritual masters have interpreted it according to their school of thought. Lord Krishna says that the Gita is his heart. Understanding the Almighty's heart is beyond human comprehension. We comprehend it only to the extent that our minds have been developed through the grace of the sadguru, the spiritual master. Our effort is to have an overview of the Gita in eighteen days. If we delve into each shloka, even 700 days won't be sufficient to explain its 700 verses. Each word of this text, for that matter even the blank spaces between each word or line, carries hidden meaning. We need the divine vision of the sadguru to truly realise and expound upon the teachings of the Gita.

The first chapter, Arjuna 'Vishaad' Yoga, shows us the battlefield and describes Arjuna's gloom. Here, we see him run away from his duty. The second chapter, Sankhya Yoga, is the eternal philosophy or the science of this creation. The third chapter, Karma Yoga, explains the law of karma. The fourth chapter, Gyana Karma Sanyas Yoga, focuses on the renunciation of all action through wisdom. In essence, it teaches the art of letting go and offering all our actions to the Divine without getting attached to their outcomes. While the third chapter was about 'action without desire', this one is 'action without attachment'. Action is based on two factors: attachment and expectation. Transcending both leads to detachment.

When we mistake imagination for reality, we lose sight of the truth. Despite the facade of well-being, the world is plagued by stress, depression and strife. Paucity of knowledge is the root cause of suffering. The remedy lies in facing reality and accepting the truth. This chapter teaches us how to act wisely.

When treating any ailment, its right diagnosis is a must. Until the root cause is ascertained, how can one treat the illness? At times, we know what the problem is but we fail to accept it. This complicates the matter.

The Lord says, '*Sanshayatma vinashyati* (The doubtful perishes)' (Gita 4:40). And this is precisely so! We see that fake news is proliferating across the media all over the world. Blatant lies are so cleverly packaged and peddled as truth. The media, be it social media, print, electronic and now even AI to an extent, plays a role in distorting reality. As a result, a false narrative is accepted as the truth.

A lie can be embellished to look like the truth, but it is not so. One needs evidence for appropriating a lie, but the truth was, is and will remain the same. Once the seed of doubt is planted in one's psyche, it spreads like gangrene, leading to amputation. That is precisely why fact-checking is gaining traction. Truth might not be accepted today, but it will remain and shall be accepted in time. The Bhagavad Gita says, 'The creation cannot be changed according to our wishes, so let us change our perception.' We are trying to understand Gyana Karma Sanyas Yoga. Reality is absolute, not relative. Relative knowledge is shaped by the state of our consciousness, and it gives rise to false beliefs. Absolute knowledge brings maturity of thought. True enlightenment dawns when we are blessed with absolute knowledge. Now, how do we get this divine knowledge? The Lord says, 'I impart this knowledge.'

Yada yada hee dharmasya glaanirbhavati Bharata|
Abhyuthaanam adharmasya tadatmanaam srujammyaham||
(Gita 4:7)

(Whenever there is a decline in righteousness and an increase in unrighteousness, O Bharata, I manifest on earth.)

This is absolute knowledge and it manifests from the Divine.

Paritraanaya sadhunaam vinaashaaya cha dushkritam|
Dharma sansthaapanaarthaya sambhavaami yugey yugey||
(Gita 4:8)

(For the protection of the good and the destruction of the evil, to establish righteousness, I manifest in every age.)

The Lord further says:

Evam paramparaapraptam imam rajarshayo viduhu|
Sa kaaleneha mahata yogo nashtaha Parantapa||
(Gita 4:2)

(This knowledge has been passed down through the
ages by succession to sages.)

This knowledge comes from me alone, just as clouds absorb water from the ocean, giving it in the form of rivers like the Ganga, Yamuna, Kaveri, etc. I manifest assuming different forms and impart this knowledge. Who can understand this knowledge?

The Lord says:

Sa evaayam muhya yogaha proktaha puratanaha|
Bhaktoasi mey sakha cheti rahasyam hyeduttamam||
(Gita 4:3)

(This ancient yoga is being taught by me because you are my
foremost devotee and friend; it is the supreme secret.)

Unconditional surrender makes us worthy of receiving this divine knowledge. It means being eager, enthusiastic, fully committed and having unwavering faith. This is how we prepare ourselves to gain divine knowledge. A true devotee will understand this: '*Tadviddhi pranipattena pariprashnena sevaya* (Approach your spiritual master surrendering unto him)' (Gita 4:34). Being curious, eager to learn, and asking again and again is the way forward. 'Gyanasinehaiva vivrakna mohah'—wisdom destroys moha (attachment), leading us to divine light. When this light illumines our consciousness, our actions become an act of worship.

A reckless act turns into regret, whereas a thoughtful act brings joy. Our action can only be deemed to be an act of yagya (sacrifice) when we are detached from the action as well as the result. This only happens when we dedicate it to a higher purpose, thereby freeing ourselves from the attachment. A selfless act, sans any ego and attachment, becomes a yagya. Here, Lord Krishna discusses twelve types of yagya.

1. **Deva Yagya:** All pujas offered to the deities or gods are Deva Yagyas. Shrimad Bhagavatam states that each sensory organ

is presided over by one deity. Shrimad Bhagavad Gita and Shrimad Bhagavatam are complementary texts, and studying them encourages a deeper understanding of the eternal philosophical truths. Our hands become instruments when they engage in acts of worship or servitude to the Divine. The beautiful verses we recite in praise of Lord Krishna are offerings to the deity of speech, Vak Devata. Similarly, when we choose to see beauty and focus on the good in others rather than their faults, it is a form of worship to the deity of vision, Drishti Devata.

2. **Brahma Yagya:** Also referred to as 'Vishaya Yoga Yagya', this happens when we dedicate ourselves selflessly to the Supreme Self. Whenever we eat, we must do it with reverence and dedication, that is, first offer it to the Divine and then consume it.

3. **Indriya Yagya:** We should not be enslaved by our senses. Are the senses subservient to us, or is it vice versa? Gopal, the ultimate controller of the senses, finds fulfilment only through the gopis.

> *Gobhih indriyai Krishna Rasam pibati iti Gopi|*
> (Shrimad Bhagavata Mahapurana 10th Canto)

(The sensory organs engrossed in absorbing Shree Krishna Rasa Amrit are the gopis).

Recite the name of Hari, listen to his glory with your ears.
Bow your head to Hari, the source of all virtues.
Perform actions with your hands for Hari, and circumambulate with your feet.
Look at Shree Jagannath with your eyes and offer yourself completely.

4. **Mano Yagya:** Are we slaves to our mind, or is the mind our slave? Mano Yagya entails being engrossed in the service of Lord Krishna and offering the ablutions of good thoughts in the fire of knowledge ignited in our mind.

5. **Dravya Yagya:** We can either spend wealth on ourselves, on other, or just squander it away. When we use the money for welfare, it is Dravya Yagya.

6. **Tapo Yagya:** Enduring life's hardships and patiently practising spiritual austerities is Tapo Yagya.

7. **Yoga Yagya:** Pranayama is Yoga Yagya. The meetings of Shree Hanuman and Vibhishana, or of Vidura and Uddhava, hold profound significance and need to be understood with care. When saintly beings meet, it becomes a Yoga Yagya. Just as physical practices such as pranayama, asana and meditation are forms of yajna—offerings made at the levels of body, mind, intellect and soul—the coming together of pure-hearted beings is a spiritual sacrifice.

8. **Swadhyaya Yagya:** Read what is important. '*Swadhyayat ma pramaditavyam* (Do not be lazy in self-study)' (Taittiriya Upanishad). Introspect and stay alert.

9. **Gyana Yagya:** We say, '*Shrimad Bhagavata Katha Gyana Yajna*' (The Shrimad Bhagwat Katha is known as a Gyana Yagna, an offering of knowledge). It is the yagya of knowledge through self-study and discourses. Parikshit Maharaj and Arjuna perform this. Following their footsteps, we are trying to do these eighteen chapters over eighteen days.

10. **Prana Yagya:** Our breathing is a yagya. When the external breath merges with the internal breath, and vice versa, each breath becomes a yagya.

11. **Atmasamyam Yagya:** To practise self-restraint is Atmasamyam Yagya.

12. **Deha Yagya:** Keeping the body healthy is a form of yagya.

13. **Prema Yagya:** When the source of love is unselfish—Anyabhilashita shoonyam—it is Prema Yajna. Shreemann Mahaprabhu Ji (Chaitanya Mahaprabhu) is the initiator of this yagya.

Premgali ati saankree, yaimey duina samaay|
(Kabir)

(The lane of divine love is very narrow; two people cannot enter here.)

Therefore, in this chapter, he explains Karma Yoga and how to detach from it. He reveals extraordinary truths and concludes with the following:

Yoga-sannyasta-karmaanam gyana-sachhinna-samshayam|
Atmavantam na karmaani nibadhnanti Dhananjaya||
(Gita 4:41)

(O Dhananjaya, the one who has renounced all actions in the self through yoga and destroyed all doubts through knowledge, is truly dedicated to the self and is not bound by actions.)

By awakening discrimination, and detaching ourselves from actions and offering them to God, we embody the essence of these thirteen yagyas. Narayanayeti samarpayami is when we offer all our actions at the Lotus Feet of Lord Krishna, and we are freed from the bondage of actions. A person who controls their inner senses is never bound by the trappings of karma. Action without agency—meaning, without attachment to the action or the sense of 'I am the doer'—can only be relinquished when we are free from disbelief and act with wisdom and discernment. Only then does action become a true act of yagna (sacrifice).

SUMMARY

Verses 1–17:   Describe the nature of Karma Yoga, the reason for the Divine's avatar and the divinity of his actions and leela.

Verses 18–23:   Divine knowledge cannot be affected by our actions.

Verses 24–30:   Discuss twelve types of yagya.

Verses 31–37:   Explain that the completeness of sacrifice is in discrimination.

Verses 38–42:   Praises of Gyana Yoga and Karma Yoga, encouragement to attain divine knowledge.

KEY QUOTES

1. Ignorance is misery.
2. Act intelligently.
3. Unconditionally surrender to the Supreme Self.
4. We should master our senses.
5. Our actions should be a source for awakening.
6. The creation cannot be changed; we need to change our perception.
7. There is a difference between theory and the dynamics of life.
8. When discrimination arises, attachment goes.

5

Karma Sanyas Yoga

The Yoga of Renunciation of Action

Total verses: 29

In our study of the Bhagavad Gita, we will now turn to the fifth chapter. It signifies the combination of action and its renunciation. Although it sounds contradictory, it involves living a life of active renunciation. Put simply, to act without attachment and any expectations whatsoever. This synthesis is crucial to understanding why this chapter is called Karma Sanyas Yoga. The teachings offer a profound philosophical discussion on the nature of action, inaction and renunciation. Unless we interpret and practise these profound teachings correctly in our lives, the Gita will simply remain a book.

In the fourth chapter, we saw that the biggest mistake one can commit is to interpret any situation without knowing its reality. When one acts without thinking, it complicates matters, giving rise to unnecessary confusion and misery. Lord Krishna, out of his sheer compassion, comes to awaken us repeatedly. He says,

'Dharma sansthaapanaarthaya sambhavaami yugey yugey (To establish dharma or righteousness, I come again and again)' (Gita 4:8). He clarifies to Arjuna why he is the chosen one: *'Bhaktosi mey sakha cheti rahasyam hyetaduttamam* (You are my devotee and a dear friend, so I am sharing this profound secret, for it is in your ultimate interest)' (Gita 4:3). To attain or acquire wisdom, one has to be humble and approach the guru with devotion: *'Tadviddhi pranipaattena pariprashnena sevaya* (The only way to learn it is to reverentially approach our spiritual master)' (Gita 4:34).

Karma Sanyas Yoga teaches us to live fully engaged in the world by performing actions sincerely and diligently while maintaining a detached attitude. Lord Krishna makes it clear that renunciation is not inactivity but about abandoning selfish desires and the ego that binds us to the endless cycle of life and death. Goswami Tulsidas says in the Ramacharitmanas: *'Udaaseen nita raheeya Gossain* (Remain detached)'. Arjuna is still somewhat confused because in the previous chapter, Lord Krishna goads him to act, and now he is suddenly talking of sanyas. Therefore, he requests Lord Krishna to explain such profound things in simpler words and show him the path he needs to follow.

Sanyasam karmana Krishna punaryogam cha shansasi|
Yachshreya yetayorekkam ttanmey broohi sunishchittam||
(Gita 5:1)

(O Krishna! You praise the renunciation of actions as well as the yoga of action. Please tell me, which is better for me?)

We are constantly finding ourselves under pressure: seeking higher education, a highly paid job, higher profits, a good spouse, successful children, and all comforts and luxuries one can imagine. The Gita is an encyclopaedia that contains answers and solutions for every problem or aspect of our lives. Today, we use a GPS while commuting between places, but I like to call the Gita our LPS, the Life Positioning System. Wisdom or discretion should be our guiding light on the path of truth. One who commands is not a guru; instead, the one who imparts wisdom is the true teacher. Jagatguru Lord Krishna bestows this divine wisdom to Arjuna. Through him, we too benefit.

These days, we remain unaware of our true purpose and are only running after the means. It is like walking backwards; we are moving, but in the wrong direction. We all have desires, but not all desires can be fulfilled. We seek happiness, which is also elusive. We all strive for success and endure hardships, yet the goal seems distant. After all, if one knows beforehand that success is impossible, why would one even try? However, what we perceive as success is not how Lord Krishna defines it. According to him, success means performing our duty to the best of our ability, without attachment to the outcome. The essence of Karma Sanyas Yoga is to act without an iota of ego and offer the fruits of our actions to the Divine. When an action is performed without a sense of doership, we take steps towards detachment. If one visits the temple or offers sewa for a selfish motive, he will serve as long as his desires are fulfilled. But when the service is performed only for the pleasure of Shree Radha Raman Lal Ji, it becomes an act of devotion and produces divine bliss. Therefore, eliminating selfishness is essential for spiritual upliftment.

In the third chapter, Lord Krishna states that humans have the unique capability to perform yagyas because they can practise renunciation, and the scriptures declare that renunciation leads to liberation. This helps individuals discover the purpose of their life.

Emotional fulfilment can only be achieved when we practise oneness. We treat others either as partners, opponents, collaborators or competitors. Oneness will establish peace and brotherhood that the world desperately needs.

So, our actions should be performed without attachment and with a feeling of oneness. *'Jeevera swarupa hoya nitya Krishna dasa*

(The true form of the Jeeva is that he is the eternal servitor of Shree Krishna).' Why can't we think that we are devotees of Shree Krishna, and all others are our brothers and sisters? From the spiritual perspective, *we are all one.*

> *Matrivat para-daareshu para-dravyeshu kaashthavat|*
> *Atmavat sarva-bhuteshu yah pashyati sa panditaha||*
> (Chanakya Niti)

(The one who views other women as mothers, others' wealth as a lump of clay, and all beings as his own, is a Pandit.)

Describing the concept of oneness, Shree Chaitanya Mahaprabhu said, 'I am neither a Brahmin, nor a Kshatriya, neither a Vaishya, nor a Shudra. I am neither a householder, nor a hermit and nor a renunciate. I am the servant of the servant of the servant of the Lotus Feet of Lord Krishna, who is the lover of the gopis, and an ocean of nectar and supreme bliss.' We should learn to see the divinity in every living being so that the feeling of brotherhood can flourish.

Sankhya philosophy, the science of cosmic evolution, describes the space contained within a pot as 'Ghattakaasha' and the space outside the pot as 'Pattakaasha'. When the pot breaks, the space inside merges with the space outside—the phenomenon of oneness!

Simply explained, renunciation means to give up the attachment to material possessions, relationships and the outcomes that arise while we fulfil our responsibilities. What we leave physically is known as tyag, and what we leave from within—without making any extra effort to leave it or the desire for it—is known as vairag. Not accepting anything from anyone may be good, but unless the thought of accepting or rejecting disappears, it is not renunciation. Gautama Buddha renounced the Shakya kingdom of Kapilavastu and became a monk. He is an embodiment of renunciation. Nothing attracted him after he embraced a monastic life. Man has immense capabilities: *Ayogya purusho naasti, yojakastatra durlabhaha* (There is none who is incapable, but rare is the one who knows the right application of his capability) (Subhashita). We need to see and accept the world as it is. The problem lies with our perception, not the world. If our face becomes dirty, we need to wash it. Wiping the mirror is foolishness. Similarly, changing the world is impossible, but changing oneself is easily possible.

Situations can either be challenging or favourable. However, if the challenge is understood and acted upon diligently, it becomes a stepping stone for growth. How we react depends on our mental make-up. A dog barks and bites, but do we bark and bite the dog? Maturity of thought and action is important.

Contentment breeds dispassion, and dispassion leads to renunciation. Let us begin with practical baby steps: remove all unwanted items from the wardrobe, unnecessary papers from the desk and unwanted emails from the inbox, and exit unnecessary groups on WhatsApp. Next, purge unwanted thoughts and worries from your mind. Our intellect should be trained to differentiate between the permanent and the temporary. Lord Krishna advises Arjuna not to grieve for the transitory aspects of life. He teaches us the art of intelligent waste disposal, which is important for both the worlds, within and without. The truth is permanent; we should focus on that. So, the first step is to perform physical actions dispassionately and wisely. Next is to emote with oneness. Finally, intellectual action must be accompanied by a strong understanding of what is permanent and what is temporary. Together, they will lead to renunciation, making us karma yogins. Lord Krishna is talking about Karma Sanyas Yoga, and it means liberating oneself from the sense of doership.

Sanyasaha karmayogascha nihishreyas karavubhau|
Tayostu karmasanyasat karmayogo vishishyattey||
(Gita 5:2)

(Sanyas and Karma Yoga both lead to the highest good,
but of the two, Karma Yoga is superior to Karma Sanyas.)

Lord Krishna is not asking us to stop all actions; instead, he wants us to do our duty meticulously with a feeling of detachment. Two things become important: having a higher purpose and freeing ourselves from the thought of doership. Our actions must benefit not only our household but also society at large. Surrendering unto Shree Radha Raman Lal, we say, 'We will become whatever you want and will go wherever you send us.'

The ultimate objective is to find the right balance between action and renunciation, while living the life of a householder, with complete detachment. Consider the example of a fisherman who casts the net to catch fish. The intelligent fish swim away, avoiding the bait altogether. A few struggle and manage to escape. Others try but fail to free themselves. Ultimately, the majority who get caught resign to their fate, unaware of the consequences. Like the fish, there are four categories of men.

- The first, ever free, is the gyani.
- The next category is the sanyasi.
- The third is the yogi.
- The entrapped one is the bhogi, caught in the net of maya.

Lord Krishna first instructs us to perform our duty, then guides us to renounce our attachment to the action. Now, He readies us to move higher towards complete detachment. This can be achieved by detaching oneself not only from actions but also from the fruits of those action. Through our actions, we are to practise renunciation to experience everlasting peace and spiritual growth.

Lord Krishna grants us the freedom to engage fully in life, yet move towards inner peace. He cautions us that the renunciation of actions is rather challenging and can only be practised by those whose minds are pure and unwavering. This purity of mind can only be achieved with devotion. So, Karma Yoga is prescribed for the masses, whereas Karma Sanyas Yoga is for a select few. Renunciation is not life-denying; it is life-enabling. We should practise oneness, for all living beings are part of this creation and are devotees of God: *'Jeevera swarupa hoya nitya Krishna dasa.'*

Shree Krishna describes Karma Sanyas Yoga as a path that must be practised by controlling the mind, intellect and senses, supported by performing austerities. This chapter reconciles the path of selfless action and renunciation, showing us that when both are pursued with the right understanding, it leads to the ultimate goal of attaining liberation. Renunciation does not entail leading the life of a recluse. Rather, it is about living in the material world with a spirit of inclusion, and weeding out all that is an impediment to leading a fulfilled life. Through meditation and self-control, we transcend illusions and realise our eternal self. This opens the doors to realisation. Discerning the permanent and temporary leads to enlightenment, and that is Karma Sanyas Yoga.

SUMMARY

Verses 1–7: Unity of Sankhya Yoga and Karma Yoga, and the importance of karma.
Verses 8–12: Attitude towards action.
Verses 13–15: The definition of a wise person.
Verses 16–21: The path to enlightenment.
Verses 22–26: Qualifications for meditation.
Verses 27–29: Recognition through meditation.

KEY QUOTES

1. The guru does not command; he imparts wisdom.
2. The upliftment of action is only possible when no selfish motive is attached.
3. Prosperity comes from welfare.
4. Success can only be achieved through renunciation.

5. Actions should be accompanied by renunciation, and emotions by oneness.
6. Only humans can forgive.
7. The teachings of the Bhagavad Gita need to be practised.
8. Renunciation is bliss.
9. The essence of Karma Sanyas Yoga is to discriminate between the permanent and the temporary, perform selfless actions for a greater purpose and liberate oneself from the sense of doership.
10. Every action has an equal and opposite reaction.
11. Rise above selfish motives.
12. Having a higher objective imparts tremendous strength.

6

Dhyan Yoga

The Yoga of Meditation or Atma Sanyama Yoga

Total verses: 47

The Bhagavad Gita discusses the four yogas: Karma Yoga, Raj Yoga, Bhakti Yoga and Gyana Yoga. The first six chapters focus on the knowledge of the true nature of the self, which can be attained through right actions. This is the prerequisite for worship. Jagatguru Shree Krishna is leading Arjuna step by step towards the ultimate goal of self-realisation. The fifth chapter teaches us to renounce our actions by performing them with detachment and selflessness. We can practise Karma Yoga by letting go of the pride that comes with a 'doer' mindset, thereby moving towards Karma Sanyas. As such, while every word of the Gita demands complete attention this chapter, Dhyan Yoga or Atma Sanyam Yoga, requires special attention because this is the yoga of meditation or self-discipline centred on self-control.

Yoga is now very much in vogue, but this is not the same as the yoga of meditation. Yoga comprises certain physical and mental exercises which prepare us for meditation. Dhyan means meditation, and it is the seventh limb of Ashtanga Yoga, following dharana, that is, concentration. Concentration precedes meditation, as deep and sustained focus leads to samadhi. 'Dhyana' is derived from 'dhi' and 'yana'. 'Dhi' is to perceive, and 'yana' is the path. Therefore, dhyana means the path of reflection. Another interesting interpretation links dhyana to the root 'dhyai', which means to think or contemplate, bringing us to a meditative state. This is one of the most profound chapters of the Gita, where Arjuna's consciousness is elevated. His inner conflict has been resolved in the previous chapter, and now Lord Krishna takes him from action to contemplation. Dhyana Yoga can be divided into three parts:

1. Concentration of the mind or control over the vagaries of the mind.
2. Control of the life source to aid the meditation practice.
3. Equanimity.

Apart from these three, abhyasa (practice) and vairagya (dispassion) are also important for meditation.

At first, we need to identify the source within and then manoeuvre it towards realisation. If we utilise it optimally, we will succeed. Man has immense potential, but needs to know how to tap it. India has infinite knowledge contained in divine texts like the Gita, Bhagavat and other scriptures. It has provided great contemplative thought for the world to ponder for ages. The world has much to offer materially, while India is a spiritual powerhouse. When these two combine, there will be heaven on earth.

Abiding peace is not found outside; it resides within. Once, a sage was delivering a discourse in Japan when the area was struck by an earthquake. As the ground trembled, all the listeners ran out. A few moments later, when the tremors subsided, the people came back and asked the sage, 'We all ran away, but how did you remain unmoved?' The sage replied, 'I also ran, the only difference was that you all ran out, whereas I ran within, where there was no earthquake!' This is the essence of meditation. It is the shifting of our focus from the outside to the inside—shifting from the body to the mind, from the mind to the intellect, from the intellect to the soul and from the soul to the Supreme Soul. The body, mind and intellect are all external. The true self lies within. In the Dhruv Stuti, when Shree Narayana appears before the child Dhruv, he freezes! The Lord touched Dhruv's cheek with his conch, and the very first word Dhruv Ji Maharaj uttered was, *'Yo'ntaha pravishya muma vaachamimaam prasuptaam* (O Lord! Can you enter my innermost being and reside in my heart? My body, mind and intellect are seeing you, but please make my soul your abode)' (Bhagavat 4:9:6).

We are all made of two elements, matter and soul. The matter—mind, intellect and the body—is ever-changing, whereas the soul is eternal. Shrimad Bhagavatam begins with the verse, *'Satyam Param Dheemahi'*. It does not say 'I pray'. Instead, it says, 'I meditate.' When a devotee speaks to God, it is a prayer, and when God speaks to the devotee, it becomes meditation. Shrimad Bhagavatam is the outpouring of Shree Veda Vyasa's meditation.

Focusing on external objects is the act of concentration, and focusing on internal objects is the act of meditation. When there are two, concentration is needed; when there is one, meditation is needed, moving us on to samadhi. The gopis were immersed in Shree Krishna all the time. Our efforts should not be self-centred. They must rise above personal gain and be pure and divine for general welfare. Practising meditation will calm the mind and lead us to self-realisation. Maharishi Patanjali is the principal teacher of yoga or Yogiraj, Lord Shiva is the Adi Yogi and Shree Krishna is Yogeshwar. Patanjali says, *'Chitteka taanata dhyanam* (The concentration of the mind is meditation).' However, meditation cannot happen without concentration. In the first verse of the

Shikshashtaka, Shree Chaitanya Mahaprabhu explains meditation as, '*Cheto-darpana maarjanam* (Cleanse the mirror of the chitta)'. Unless the mirror is clean, the image in it will not be clear. Chanting God's name or singing Divine glories cleanses the mind.

Consider it this way. There are four layers: first is the body, behind it is the mind, then comes the intellect, followed by the ego. By overcoming these, we reach consciousness. Immersing the mind in God or meditating on God is the first step. Patanjali adds, '*Yoga chitta-vritti nirodhah* (The cessation of the fluctuations of the mind and the concentration of consciousness is meditation).' A craftsman sitting by the roadside was immersed in making arrows, and Bhagwan Dattatreya was watching him attentively. At that moment, the king's grand procession of elephants, horses and soldiers passed by, beating their drums and blowing bugles. The man remained unmoved and continued sharpening his arrows. Admiring his single-minded focus, he made him his guru, and he learnt about concentration.

The first nine verses of this chapter explain Ashtanga Yoga. The Patanjali Yoga Sutras also give a detailed description of Ashtanga Yoga; however, we will discuss it briefly to understand the concept. Mastering the first six limbs of yoga and learning to apply yama and niyama (control and restrictions) in daily life will enhance our dhyana. It enables practitioners to become free of samskaras, or tendencies of the mind. During dharana, practitioners still encounter distractions. The focus is not always continuous, but with constant practice, the mind gradually becomes steady. When this focus is uninterrupted, it is dhyana. Unlike dharana, which is connected to the object of meditation, dhyana is about becoming one with the object in a calm state. It is a state of mind where is only a single idea remains. In dhyana, our awareness withdraws from all other things, and the mind merges with the object of meditation. As we progress, we become aware of only the self and the object of meditation. It is a state of stilling the mind with clear self-awareness. At this stage, all other samskaras disappear. It is, essentially, merging with the object of our focus that began in dharana. So, for example, if the object in dharana was a candle flame, in dhyana, practitioners feel completely one with the flame. Shree Krishna now begins explaining the steps leading to meditation.

Aarurukshor muniryogam Karma karanmuchyatey|
Yogarudhasya tasyaiva shamaha karanmuchyatey||
(Gita 6:3)

(Work is said to be the cause for a sage who seeks to scale the peak of yoga; as regards this very sage who has scaled it, quiescence is said to be the cause.)

From verses 1 to 4, Lord Krishna explains the concept of a yogarurukshu, comprising yama, niyama, asana and pranayama. Verses 5 to 9 explain the concept of a yogaarudha, which explains pratyahara, dharana, dhyana and samadhi, practised by one who can now dismount his steed, having reached the end of his journey. These are the eight principles of Ashtanga Yoga. Step by step, Lord Krishna guides us through the preparatory disciplines and the disqualifications for meditation. This is followed by the test of enlightenment. A realised soul feels one with all of creation. He doesn't worship God only in a temple or a church or a mosque, but in every living being, abiding in the atman. It is meaningless to declare love for God when we cannot connect with His living images all around us. Yogarurukshu is about:

1. **Yama:** These should not be done.
   - Ahimsa (non-violence): Our actions should be non-violent: '*Ahimsa paramo dharma* (Non-violence is the highest dharma).' However, non-violence does not mean being passive.
   - Satya (truthfulness): *Satyam param dheemahi* (the purest form of God is truth).
   - Asteya: Do not steal.

- Brahmacharya: Control the senses.
- Aparigraha: Do not possess or claim ownership over anything.
2. **Niyama:** These should be done.
   - Shaucha: Do what is right with purity.
   - Santosha: Be content.
   - Tapas: Perform austerities.
   - Swadhyaya: Engage in self-study.
   - Ishvara pranidhana: Seek and surrender to the Almighty.
3. **Asana:** The Lord says, '*Shuchau deshe pratishthapya* (Sit in a clean place).' The word 'shuchau' has been used because it denotes purity and sanctity. If the place is dirty or has a foul smell with ants crawling all over, meditation will be impossible. Originally, there were 8.4 million types of asanas. Over time, this number was reduced to eighty-four, and now to thirty-two prominent ones. In other words, sit in a clean place comfortably, where concentration becomes easy.
4. **Pranayama:** This is the control of the breath. The practice helps you connect your inner and outer worlds. The Yoga Sutras describe eight types of pranayama:
   - Surya Bhedan (sun-piercing breath)
   - Ujjayi (victorious breath)
   - Sheetkari (hissing breath)
   - Sheetali (cooling breath)
   - Bhastrika (bellows breath)
   - Bhramari (bee breath)
   - Moorchha (fainting breath)
   - Plavini (floating breath)

   Verses 5 to 9 explain 'Yogaarudha'.
5. **Pratyahara:** When the mind wanders, bringing it back under control is yoga. There are four types:
   - Indriya Pratyahara relates to the senses.
   - Prana Pratyahara relates to the life force.
   - Karma Pratyahara relates to action.

- Manas Pratyahara relates to the mind.
6. **Dharana:** This involves fixing the mind and giving the mind a suitable object for concentration. There are four types explained in the Yoga Sutras:
   - Vitarka (dense)
   - Vichara (subtle)
   - Ananda (bliss)
   - Asmita (individuality)

   Going beyond these four, the fifth stage lacks an object, and only the attention on the latent impressions remains.
7. **Dhyana:** This is total concentration.
   - Gurupara Dhyana relates to the guru.
   - Atmapara Dhyana relates to the soul.
   - Brahmapara Dhyana relates to Brahman, the Supreme Personality of Godhead.
8. **Samadhi:** This is the highest state of meditation. There are two types of samadhi.
   - Sabeeja Samadhi is of two types:
     - Sampragnata: savitarka, savichara.
     - Asampragnata: nirvitarka, nirvichara.
   - Nirbeeja Samadhi is of two types: dharma and medha

So, Lord Krishna has explained the practice of meditation as the final gateway to self-realisation. It is the highest spiritual discipline to be practised diligently and devotedly with the help of qualified practitioners. A prerequisite of meditation is a calm mind, free of desires and attachments. Shree Krishna defines a sanyasi as one who does what should be done, fulfilling his duties and responsibilities without worrying about the fruits of his actions. He has elaborately described this entire concept. At the beginning of this chapter, he explains the characteristics of a yogi and a renunciate. Who is a yogi? One who is united with the Lord. Who is a renunciate? One who is detached from maya. In a way, detachment from maya is in itself a connection with the Divine. However, the yogi is superior because he is directly connected with the Lord. Renunciation does not mean giving up; it means acceptance. One need not don ochre clothes to become a sanyasi or push away any worldly enjoyment to be spiritual. All that is needed is a change of mindset.

Verses 10–15, 16–23 and 24–27 describe sadhana, while verses 15, 23 and 27 describe siddhi. Verses 27 to 32 talk about the distinction between Brahman, Paramatman and Bhagavan. That which exists everywhere is Brahman. For example, electricity can be generated from water, but water has no qualities or shape of its own. When a dynamo is connected, electricity is generated. When it passes through a bulb, it emits light. So, Brahman is universal, while Paramatman is the supreme soul residing in all living beings. The third aspect is Bhagavan, the Supreme Personality of Godhead or God, endowed with qualities and a form.

From verses 33 to 36, Arjuna talks about his mind, saying:

Chanchalam hi manah Krishna pramaathi balavadriddham|
Tasyaham nigraham manye vayor iva sudushkaram||
(Gita 6:34)

(O Krishna! The mind is very restless, turbulent, strong and obstinate.
I think controlling it is as difficult as controlling the wind.)

In verses 37 to 42, Arjuna asks what will happen if he fails and is unable to follow Lord Krishna's instructions. The Lord very sweetly responds:

Asanshayam maha-baho mano durnigraham chalam|
Abhyasena tu Kaunteya vairagyena cha grihyattey||
(Gita 6:35)

(O mighty-armed one, undoubtedly the mind is difficult to
control and restless, but with practice and detachment,
it can be controlled.)

Arjuna is afraid of stepping beyond the safe boundaries of his present existence to discover the unknown realm of the infinite. He asks Lord Krishna about the fate of those who commit themselves to a spiritual life but die before its realisation. Shree Krishna gives a fitting reply to reveal one of the most insightful laws of life. He says, 'One who is righteous never comes to grief. Either now or in the future. Your efforts will not go in vain. You will carry forward the credits to your next life.' A spiritually evolved person who falls short of realisation will either be born in a wealthy and happy family or as a yogi. Endowed with enriching wisdom acquired in previous lives, he will strive once again to attain enlightenment.

In verses 43 to 47, Lord Krishna describes the subtleties of a yogi who has attained the highest state.

Yoginam api sarvesham madgatey anantar-atmana|
Shraddhavan bhajattey yo maam sa mey yuktatamo mataha||
(Gita 6:47)

(Of all yogis, the one with faith, who always abides in me,
thinks of me within himself and worships me,
is considered by me to be one with me in yoga.)

In this way, Lord Krishna lays the foundation for the next chapter, transitioning from Ashtanga Yoga to the mind, and from the mind to the Supreme Consciousness. If we remain calm—illustrated by the lamp analogy given by Him—just as placing a glass over a lamp protects it from the external wind, the Gita shields our inner light and prevents external elements from disturbing us.

Dhyana Yoga teaches us that what we see from the surface, this, like our body, runs very deep. Similarly, when we look at the ocean from above, we cannot judge how deep it is. The disturbance is only on the surface. The deeper we go, the calmer it becomes. No matter how many rivers flow into the water, it never floods. A realised soul is like the ocean, calm and serene.

I pray that we become like the ocean. We take time to figure out new gadgets or services like GPS because we know that if the it doesn't work, we won't reach our destination. So, if we don't understand it in one day, we spend ten days trying to get a grasp of it. Similarly, we must also understand our LPS, the Life Positioning System, to reach the ultimate goal in life.

Thus, Lord Krishna assures us that the path to everlasting peace and happiness is a life of truth. He concludes that the yogi is superior to an ascetic, a gyani and a karmi. The highest among all the yogis is one who engages in bhakti. This chapter is a deep dive into mastering self-control and balance. These teachings are not restricted to a particular faith or era but are universally applicable to our everyday life. Implementing the principles of Karma Yoga, maintaining equilibrium, harnessing the power of meditation, practising equality and compassion, and developing self-control will strengthen our mental peace and improve the quality of our life. In essence, it is an invitation to self-reflection, self-regulation and self-transcendence, encapsulating a profound philosophy that goes beyond religion and reaches the realm of spirituality. *Add whatever you need to your consciousness from this. I am giving you the seed; you must water it to grow!*

SUMMARY

Verses 1–9:	Explanation of both parts of Ashtanga Yoga: Yogarurukshu and Yogaarudha.
Verses 10–15:	The description of sadhana.
Verses 16–26:	The description of siddhi.
Verses 27–32:	The distinction between Brahman, Paramatman and Bhagavan.
Verses 33–36:	The description of the restlessness of the mind and the fate of an unsuccessful yogi.

Verses 37–42:   The description of the yogi.
Verses 43–47:   The explanation of a devotee.

KEY QUOTES

1. The Bhagavad Gita is a subject of deep contemplation.
2. Human life contains infinite possibilities.
3. A noble purpose and a practical path are two fundamental elements of life.
4. Shift the focus from unreliable things to reliable ones.
5. Renunciation is not about giving up anything; it is about acceptance.
6. One should dive within oneself.
7. Redeem yourself on your own. Nobody else can help you.
8. Those who do good never suffer, but the selfish are destroyed.

7

Gyana Vigyan Yoga

Adhyatma Yoga

Total verses: 30

The Bhagavad Gita consists of eighteen chapters. The great masters have divided them into set of six, each called Shatakam. The first set is called Shodhana, meaning inquiry; the second is Bodhana, meaning teaching; and the third is Sadhana, meaning the technique. In the Shodhana Shatakam, we enquire about the atman, anatma, paramatman, karma, dhyana, etc. In the second, the teachings begin from the seventh chapter. The Gita is conceptualised as a question-and-answer-based discourse between Arjuna and Shree Krishna. The uniqueness of this chapter lies in the fact that Arjuna does not question but is attentively listening to the Lord. In the learning process, certain facts must be understood and accepted without questioning. Before we begin, we need to study the difference between gyana (knowledge) and vigyan (experiential knowledge). Shree Krishna explains the importance of gyana, its application and the experiential knowledge of oneness. In the previous chapter, He said that amongst all the yogis, the one who resides in him and serves the universe with devotion is dear to him.

In the first six chapters, Shree Krishna has shared all the knowledge required for a person to elevate themselves from the material realm to the heights of perfection. After receiving the knowledge, one must ponder over it and convert it into wisdom. There is a significant gap between knowing and doing. We strive to speak the language of wisdom, but we often fail to apply the knowledge we have to overcome life's challenges and emerge victorious. To accomplish this, we need to follow Shravana, Manana and Nidhidhyasana. Knowledge is first read or heard from the guru, followed by reflection. This involves contemplating and studying it from different angles. Only then does knowledge become integrated into our system. Once internalised, we begin to live it. Then comes meditating upon it, which leads us to self-realisation. In this chapter, Lord Krishna bridges the gap between knowing and doing by enforcing reflection. He presents the knowledge from a fresh perspective, igniting original thinking. He imparts wisdom infused with devotion to convert theory into practice. Shree Krishna begins this with an analysis of the world and shows how the Brahman permeates the universe. As humans, we can choose between staying with the world or moving towards the spirit. Pursue limited, myopic goals, or rise above the obvious and seek the Eternal. The choice is ours, and He guides us towards the right direction and ensures we reach the goal. All paths eventually lead to Him alone.

The Gita's teachings are profound, with countless commentaries and interpretations available to different approaches in understanding. I believe that the Gita is best explored under the guidance of a teacher. We develop this understanding when the Divine and the Gita both bless us. Mahatma Gandhi famously referred to the Gita as his 'eternal mother' and Lord Krishna himself declares that the Gita is his heart, *'Gita mey hridayam Partha.'*

Therefore, to understand the purport, we must approach it with reverence. Bhakti essentially means forming a relationship with the Divine and surrendering unto Him.

Lord Krishna explains the tenets of bhakti to Arjuna. This same teaching will be summarised later in the eighteenth chapter from verses 46 to 54. It is established in the Vedanta texts that worship done with loving devotion constitutes the means of attaining the Divine. These texts affirm that dhyana and upasana form the path to mindfulness and thoughts centred on Lord Krishna. This flow of divine thought is only possible with the will and grace of the benevolent Lord. The material and the spiritual dimensions of His energies are explained by him herein. He clarifies that, just like the beads strung together on a thread, all energies have originated from Him and rest in Him alone. Although transgressing maya is very difficult, those who surrender unto Him will cross over by his grace. In life, attaining higher qualifications is not an easy task. One needs to pass entrance examinations and go through interviews. But here, the only qualification needed is: a sincere desire and devotion. Though Dhritarastra did not qualify per se to hear Gita, he was blessed by Sanjaya's compassion. On the other hand, Arjuna, driven by his eagerness, received the flow of Lord Krishna's grace.

In the Ramayana, Lord Rama demonstrates the transformative power of grace by extending it even to the fickle-minded monkeys who helped him defeat Ravana. Some intellectuals mistakenly believe that spiritual study is reserved for old age. But the Gita is accessible to all, and its divine appeal is universal and eternal, embodying the very presence of the Divine as Shabd Brahman (the transcendental sound).

Gurudev Ravindranath Tagore once said, 'When the words come out from the depths of truth, they touch the soul.' For, in such moments, it is God speaking to God. Meditation cannot be forced; it happens naturally. When our mind merges with the cosmic mind, we experience true meditation. We reach beyond the oscillations of happiness and sorrow, success and failure. At the personal level, one seeks success and happiness. However, failure and unhappiness cannot be barred. True bliss lies beyond the dualities of the mind and intellect; it is the very nature of the soul.

Our journey, though often focused on the body, mind and intellect, should ultimately lead us inwards to the soul consciousness. The guru aids us on this journey, as he knows the way. I belong to the bhakti tradition, and expounding on bhakti comes naturally to me. I share here an overview of bhakti, which in itself is very exhaustive. The Ramayana says:

> *Eshwar ansa jeeva avinasi|*
> *Chetan amala sahaj sukh raasi||*
> (Ramcharitmanas Uttarkanda: 116)

> (The jeeva is a part of the Divine and is eternal. He is untainted consciousness and by nature joyous.)

The atman is a tiny part of the paramatman. They are both the same. Shree Krishna is the paramatman, and Arjuna represents the jeeva. In Vibhuti Yoga, Lord Krishna declares, '*Pandavanaam Dhananjaya* (Amongst the Pandavas I am Arjuna)' (Gita 10.37). The words affirm Arjuna's exalted status. Shree Chaitanya Mahaprabhu said, '*Achintya bheda-abheda* (Divine grace is beyond comprehension).' The Divine can only be understood by grace: '*Naayam atma pravachanena labhyaha* (The Divine cannot be understood by eloquent discourses).' Each soul realises God based on its individuality and to the extent God wants to reveal himself.

In the last verse of the sixth chapter, Lord Krishna says:

> *Chanchalam hee manah Krishna pramathi balavaddridham|*
> *Tasyaham nigraham mannye vaayoriva sudushkaram||*
> (Gita 6: 47)

> (The one who engages in devotion to me, engaged in hearing and chanting my name is the best.)

Meditation leads to self-realisation, but bhakti goes beyond. This can only be experienced, not explained. I might sound partial because of my natural inclination, but I leave it to individual experience. Believe me, becoming a guru is easy, but to become an able disciple is very difficult.

Here is a simple comparison between gyaan and bhakti:

Knowledge (Gyaan)	Devotion (Bhakti)
1. Knowledge has a birth, and thus will also have a death.	1. In devotion, knowledge naturally arises, and what arises naturally doesn't die.
2. Knowledge demands to be spoken.	2. Devotion demands to be listened to.
3. Knowledge is a secondary form of yoga.	3. Devotion is the primary form of yoga.
4. Knowledge cannot progress without devotion and remains limited to academic learning.	4. The subtlety of devotion begins with listening.
5. Knowledge provides experience.	5. Devotion leads to realisation.
6. The process of gaining knowledge is complex and difficult.	6. The process of devotion is simple and easy.
7. Knowledge always goes towards devotion.	7. Devotion doesn't need to go anywhere.
8. Knowledge can lead to pride.	8. Devotion brings humility and simplicity.
9. Knowledge may involve duality and delusion.	9. Devotion frees one from duality and delusion.
10. Knowledge emphasises the mind.	10. Devotion emphasises the heart.

In the first shloka of this chapter, the Lord says:

Mayyasaktamanaha Partha yogam yunjanmadashryahaha|
Asanshyam samagram maam yatha gyasasi tatshrunnu||
(Gita 7:1)

(Listen, Partha! With the mind attached exclusively to me, and surrendered to me with the practice of Bhakti Yoga, you can know me completely without doubt.)

For a better understanding, let us examine the shloka in the reverse order: '*Shrunu yatha gyasasi samagram ashanshayam madaashryaha yogam yunja mayyasaktmanaha.*' 'Shrunu' or listening is the first form of bhakti. In the Shrimad Bhagavatam, Prahalad Ji Maharaj, describing the Navadha Bhakti, the nine types of bhakti, says:

Shravannam kirtannam Vishno smarannam paadsevanam|
Archannam vandannam daasyam sakhyam aatmanivedanam||
(Shrimad Bhagavatam 7:5:23)

(Hearing and chanting the Divine names, remembering them and serving the Divine Lotus Feet. Worshipping, praying, serving and considering the Lord as the only true friend and surrendering unto Him.)

Returning to the first shloka, Lord Krishna explains that one who listens to his katha attentively attains complete understanding and secures his refuge. This marks the beginning of bhakti. Shravana bhakti is the first and the fundamental form of devotion. Interestingly, this katha enters through our ears even if we are inattentive or asleep, ready to awaken us one day.

Through Bhakti Yoga, the devotee, with the mind and intellect immersed in Lord Krishna, comes closer to Him. One meaning of Krishna is 'the one who attracts'. The Divine attracts his devotee, and, unlike worldly attractions, this spiritual attraction only grows stronger.

Whether seen or heard, the shabda is a manifestation of Brahman. It penetrates the depths of our soul and stirs us into awakening. In my view, shravana is not only the easiest but also the most powerful path to spiritual progress. As we immerse ourselves in the flow of listening, the various steps of Ashtanga Yoga unfold side by side. The second shloka says:

Gyanam tteyaham savigyanmiddam vakshyamyasheshataha|
Yajgyatva neha bhooyo anyajgyatavyam vishishyattey||
(Gita 7:2)

(I shall now reveal unto you fully this knowledge and wisdom, knowing which nothing else remains to be known.)

Lord Krishna explains that listening leads to wisdom. He differentiates between gyana and vigyan. The external is science; the internal is wisdom. It is said, *Vidya dadati vinayam* (True knowledge leads to humility) (Subhashita), but I interpret this to mean that one who is truly humble is knowledgeable.

In the following shlokas, Lord Krishna speaks of Ashtadha Prakriti, or the eightfold material nature that constitutes the outer world: earth, water, air, fire, ether, mind, intellect and ego. Regardless of whether it is outer or inner, the Divine pervades all. In the seventh shloka, Lord Krishna says:

Matta parataram nanyat kinchidasti Dhananjaya|
Mayi sarvamiddam prottam sutrey mannigana iva||
(Gita 7:7)

(There is nothing higher than me, O Arjuna. Everything rests in me as the beads strung in a mala.)

Raso ahamapsu Kaunteya prabhasmi Shashi suryayoho|
Prannavaha sarva vedeyshu shabdaha khey paurusham nrishu||
(Gita 7:8)

(I am the rasa in the water, O son of Kunti, and the radiance of the sun and the moon. I am the sacred syllable 'Om' in the Vedic mantras; I am the sound in the ether and the ability in humans.)

For the devotee, the Lord exists in everything. Shree Krishna distils these profound truths for Arjuna's understanding. If the Divine is so easy to understand, then why is He beyond comprehension? Lord Krishna answers that maya creates the barrier: '*Maameva ye prapaddyantey mayametam taranti ttey* (The surrendered souls can cross over my Maya)' (Gita 7:14). Maya is very powerful; it entangles the ignorant and those with evil tendencies. Therefore, we must continually cleanse the inner being through devotional practices and unconditionally surrender at the Lotus Feet of the Lord.

Lord Krishna further classifies the devotees in the following shloka:

Chaturvidha bhajantey maam janaha sukritinoarjuna|
Aarto jigyaasu arthaarthi gyani cha Bharatasrhabha||
(Gita 7:16)

(Arjuna, four types of people engage in devotional practices: the distressed, seekers of knowledge, those who seek wealth and the wise.)

The onus is on us to discover the quickest and most effective path to the goal of total fulfilment. The ignorant, unaware of the higher truths, pursue and obtain finite ends. A few, however, perceive that which transcends the material plane and turn to God. They belong to four categories. Some only seek to enhance their wealth. They believe that supplication to God will bestow riches. The distressed who have met with tragic circumstances seek solace. The curious ones look for answers to their questions. But the jnanis, the wise, excel. They see the futility of worldly pursuits and abide in the transcendental. Unmoved by the glitter of transitory joys, they search for permanent joy and reach enlightenment.

> *Tesham gyani nitya yukta ekbhaktir vishishyattey|*
> *Priyo hee gyaninotyartham aham sa cha mey priyaha||*
> (Gita 7:17)

(Among these, those who worship me with knowledge and surrender unto me with single-minded devotion are dear to me.)

Lord Krishna says that He eagerly awaits a person who unconditionally surrenders and tries to know Him. He goes on to say:

> *Bahoona janmanaamantey gyanvaanmam prapaddyatey|*
> *Vasudevaha sarvamiti sa mahatma sudurlabhaha||*
> (Gita 7:19)

(Practising spiritual austerities from many lives, endowed with knowledge, the one who surrenders unto me, knowing me as all that is to be known, such a mahatma is very rare.)

From verses 20 to 25, Lord Krishna explains the traits of the devotee who expects something in return for the devotion. In the following shloka, Shree Krishna describes the traits of the devotee who realises that everything belongs to the Supreme. He unconditionally surrenders to the will of the Lord.

> *Yesham tvantgatam papam jananam punyakarmanam|*
> *Ttey dvandmohanirmukta bhajantey maam dridhavrataha||*
> (Gita 7:28)

(Those whose sins have been destroyed by spiritual austerities are disillusioned. They worship me with a firm conviction.)

Bheeshma Pitamaha is an example of such a devotee who, at the last stage of his life, says: '*Iti mati roopa Kalpita vitrishna, Bhagwati saatvat pungavey vibhoonmi* (I now offer my mind, intellect and consciousness unto you, my Lord)' (Srimad Bhagavatam 1:9:32). The essence of this chapter is concentrated in just one word:

shrunu. We need to learn the art of listening. For this we need to practise maun, patience, vivek, alertness and the steps of meditation discussed previously. If we pay attention, then even one word can awaken us.

When we focus our energies on the Divine Lotus Feet of Lord Krishna, we are blessed with a glimpse of bhakti. We need to harmoniously integrate gyana and bhakti into our daily lives. Gyana Yoga emphasises intellectual understanding and the pursuit of wisdom. This path involves deep reflection, discernment and the quest for self-realisation. Bhakti Yoga, the path of devotion, teaches us to surrender and dedicate our lives to the Divine, cultivating love, compassion and faith. Bhakti fosters humility and a sense of oneness. It aligns us with higher values, leading to moral and spiritual development. Both paths are interwoven—devotion without knowledge could become blind faith, lacking discernment and depth. On the other hand, knowledge without devotion could lead to arrogance and a disconnect from the compassionate essence of the universe.

SUMMARY

Verse 1:	The introduction of Bhakti Yoga through 'shravan'.
Verse 2:	The description of gyana.
Verses 3–6:	The description of prakriti.
Verses 7–12:	The spiritual description of nature.
Verses 12–14:	Maya and its influence.
Verses 15–16:	The description of three evil and four virtuous persons.
Verses 17–18:	The description of Premi Bhakta.
Verse 19:	A rare personality.
Verses 20–25:	Sakama Bhakti.
Verses 26–28:	Nishkama Bhakti.
Verses 29–30:	The description of Yoga Nishtha.

KEY QUOTES

1. The Bhagavad Gita transforms an ordinary person into an extraordinary being.
2. We need to understand the mind to direct it towards the right path.
3. Knowledge and intelligence are educational qualifications.
4. Changing your outlook alters the creation.
5. Gyana is spoken, whereas bhakti is heard.
6. The one who is absorbed in Prema Bhakti is the best.
7. The premi is fearless.
8. Some narrate the katha, whereas some become the katha.
9. Gyana need not be exhibited; it should be understood.
10. What has already been achieved can be emulated by others.
11. We need a heart for bhakti. Emotions flow from the heart, and in order to control the flow, we need patience and wisdom.

8

Akshar Brahma Yoga

Tarak Brahma Yoga
Total verses: 28

In the eighth chapter of the Bhagavad Gita, Lord Krishna delves into the eternal nature of the soul and knowledge of the imperishable Brahman (akshara); in other words, the nature of reality and the spiritual journey. He emphasises the power of thoughts in shaping destinies and the importance of redirecting our focus from material pursuits to spiritual aspirations. By mastering the senses and embracing Karma Yoga, Bhakti Yoga and Gyana Yoga, individuals can cultivate a calm mind free of desires, paving the way for meditation and self-realisation under the guidance of able mentors. The Lord elucidates the cosmic cycle of creation and dissolution, likening it to the cyclical passage of day and night in the realm of Lord Brahma, while affirming Brahman's transcendence beyond this cosmic rhythm.

Shree Krishna offers humanity three paths to experience spiritual evolution: the path of return, wherein desire-driven noble actions lead to heavenly rewards and then reincarnation; the path of gradual liberation, where sincere spiritual endeavours result in a phased liberation through heavenly experiences before attaining higher states of consciousness; and the path of direct liberation, where individuals break free from the cycle of birth and death to achieve moksha, the ultimate liberation from worldly bondage. These teachings illuminate the transformative journey from worldly entanglement to spiritual liberation, offering profound insights into the nature of existence and the path to transcendence.

The Upanishads talk about four things: shrotavya (listening), mantavya (thinking), vaktavya (speaking) and maun (complete silence). In this state of silence, we hear the inner voice. The Bhagavad Gita reveals the nature of the Supreme Personality of Godhead and leads to the understanding of the Divine nature. Each person possesses certain good and bad qualities. The very first depiction of the Gita shows Arjuna and Shree Krishna seated on the chariot amid both the armies. One stands for virtue, and the other for vice. Man is poised between evil and noble tendencies. The Gita helps us recognise virtue, enabling us to eliminate evil. Thoughts play a very crucial role in life. We become what we think. It is very easy to point a finger at someone, but people forget that three fingers remain pointed towards themselves. Blaming feeds the ego, whereas accepting the blame eats into the ego. People want to change others without changing themselves, but the truth is that when we change, the world changes magically. Our expectations are the cause of our misery. Not expecting anything from anyone is bliss. Three tendencies abide in all of us: rajasic, tamasic and sattvic. Our nature is defined by the predominance of either of these tendencies.

Today, the gene silencing technique is being used to treat many genetic disorders. In the Bhagavad Gita, Lord Krishna performs 'guna silencing'. He suppresses the rajasic and the tamasic tendencies and enhances the sattvic traits within us. Our rishis have also divided our day in three parts. Early morning, 4–6 a.m., is sattvic. From sunrise to sunset is rajasic, and past sunset to bedtime is tamasic. Whether we desire material prosperity or spiritual accomplishment, sincerity in action, purity in the heart and clear thinking are prerequisites. We attain material comforts in life, but Lord Krishna reminds us: 'Maamupettya punarjanma dukhaalayam ashaashwatam (Having attained me, there is no rebirth in this transient world, full of miseries)' (Gita 8:15). In the first two shlokas of this chapter, Arjuna raises seven queries. He has now stepped out of delusion and become a spiritual aspirant, asking probing questions.

Kim tadbrahma kitadhyatmam kim karma Purushottama|
Adhibhootam cha kim proktam adhidaivam kimuchyattey||
Adhiyagyaha katham koatra deheyasmin Madhusudana|
Prayaankaaley cha katham gyeyosi niyataatmabhihi||
(Gita 8:1 and 8:2)

(Arjuna says, O Supreme Lord! What is Brahman? What is adhyatma? What is karma? What is adhibhuta? Who is adhidaiva? Who is adhiyagna, and how does he reside in the human body? O Krishna! How does one know you and remember you at the time of death?)

Lord Krishna answers the first six questions very simply in the next shloka, stating that the Supreme, indestructible entity is Brahman, and adhyatma is one's self. Actions related to the material personality of living beings and their development are karma. Adhibhuta is the physical manifestation that is constantly changing. Adhidaiva is the universal form of God, which presides over the celestial gods. The one who dwells in the heart of every living entity is the adhiyagna—the receiver of all sacrifices.

Shree Krishna explains the seventh question in detail. Here, he is preparing us for the ultimate reality, that is, death. We all do so much for life, which is uncertain, yet we neglect death, which is a certainty, either out of fear or sheer indifference. The Shrimad Bhagavatam begins with the contemplation of death; Siddhartha became Buddha when he understood its mystery. Death is the journey back home. Therefore, it needs to be celebrated, not mourned. We are scared to visualise the end. Lord Krishna wants to show us the reality by explaining the intricacies.

In this chapter, the subject moves from karma, sanyas and gyana to how we can reach the eternal Godhead. Shree Krishna addresses several assorted topics. At the end of the previous chapter, He introduces new terminology, which prompts Arjuna to ask for an explanation of the terms. Arjuna also asks about the sacrificial principle in the body and how one might contemplate Him at the time of death. A part of Shree Krishna's answer to the last question is enigmatic; it is unclear if the answer has to be approached literally or a figuratively. It may help to recall the final two verses of the seventh chapter, wherein He says: 'Those who, having taken refuge in me, striving for relief from old age and death, get to know that Brahman as well as the entire field of actions. Those who see me manifesting in "adhyatma", "adhibhuta", "adhidaiva" and "adhiyagna", while being yoked to the intellect even at the time of death, realise me.' These technical terms appear here for the first time in Lord Krishna's teachings and naturally elicit the question from Arjuna, who seeks a deeper explanation and wants to know how one can reach out to Him at the last stage.

The prefix 'adhi' denotes something that stands apart as the best in class. Shree Krishna offers a succinct response. Brahman is the highest, immutable and eternal. The essential nature or the conscious self, not the ego, is adhyatma. The insentient non-eternal is adhibhuta. The purusha, or the supreme spirit, is adhidaiva. Shree Krishna being immanent in one's body and partaking in the sacrificial offering is adhiyagna. In the Gita (5:29), Shree Krishna similarly declares that He is the enjoyer of all sacrifices. Similarly, in the Gita (15:14), He refers to Himself as Vaiswanara, necessary for digesting food, highlighting the fact that even the consumption of food is seen as an offering of oblations in the yagna. Karma is the process through which both sentient and insentient beings are created. Karma is the cause of all changes in the darshana. These technical terms have been elaborately interpreted by the acharyas, but for the understanding it is sufficient to stay with Shree Krishna's definitions.

Punarapi Janamam punarapi marannam punarapi Janani jatharey shayanam|
Iha sansarey bahu dustarey, kripaya paarey, paahi Murarey|
Bhaja Govindam, Bhaja Govindam, Bhaja Govindam moodhamattey||
(*Bhaja Govindam Stotra* by Adi Shankaracharya)

(The endless cycle of birth, death and entering the mother's womb, it is indeed very hard to cross this boundless ocean of misery, that is, this world. O Murari! Out of your causeless mercy please rid me from this transmigratory process.)

Lord Krishna reveals the path to cross this endless ocean of samsara (world), which is filled with miseries. The soul's hankering at the time of death determines its future. He says that when one breathes their last with the mind set on Him, the Supreme, there is no doubt that the individual will reach Him. This is a release! He adds that in contrast to predestination, whatever one is ruminating on in the final moments of life the soul will realise it. The future can be willed, at least in principle. In the fifth shloka, Lord Krishna says:

Antakaaley cha maameva smaranmuktva kallevaram|
Yaha prayaati sa madbhavam yati naastyatra sanshayaha||
(Gita 8:5)

(Whoever, at the time of death, leaves his body remembering me alone, at once attains me, without any doubt.)

Yam yam vapi smaranbhavam tyajatyatey kallevaram|
Tam tameyvaiti Kaunteya sada tadbhaavbhavitaha||
(Gita 8:6)

(Whatever state of being one remembers when he leaves the body, that state he will attain without fail.)

Tasmat sarveshu kaaleyshu maamnusmara yudhya cha|
Mayyarpita manobuddhir maameyvaishyasya sanshayam||
(Gita 8:7)

(Therefore, you should always think of me and carry out your prescribed duty as a warrior. With all your actions, mind and intellect fixed on me, you will attain me without doubt.)

Regular practice is critical. Without a continuous effort to chant the name of the Divine, it will be very difficult to remember him at the end. The jeeva is ensnared by maya, and only Divine grace can help cross over this deep crevice of illusion. The saints say, '*Shwas shwas per Krishna bhaja, vritha shwas jana khoya, arey na jaaney iss shwas kee aavani hoya na hoya* (Repeat the name of Krishna with each breath, for who knows, whether the next breath will come)?' People often ask how long they should sing a bhajan. Do as long as it doesn't become your nature. Lord Krishna clarifies:

Abhyasyoga yukteyna chetasa nanyagaamina|
Paramam purusham divyam yati Parthanuchintayann||
(Gita 8:8)

(One who mediates on me with the mind constantly remembering me, un-deviated from the path, he, O Partha, is bound to attain me.)

Mahatma Gandhi uttered 'Hey Ram' just before death. This came to him naturally, but one must remember that it entailed serious effort and practice on his part. From verses 9 to 13, Lord Krishna explains the method of securing death. This involves certain yogic practices during which the devotee focuses on the Divine, passing the seven chakras present in our body.

Ananyachetaha satatam yomaam smarati nityashaha|
Tasyaaham sulabhaha Partha nityayuktasya yoginaha||
(Gita 8:14)

(O Partha! One who remembers me without deviation attains me very easily because of the constant engagement in devotional service.)

When a jeeva has unrealised desires, it becomes fixated on them and keeps brooding over them, especially later in life, as an unfulfilled goal. This is called vasana. The vasanas shape the jeeva's future, driving it to seek fulfilment of its unfulfilled hankering, whether in this life or the next. It is therefore up to each jeeva to prepare for its desired future outcome. The example of Jadabharata who was born as a deer because of his attachment to a motherless fawn at the end of his life aptly illustrates this point.

Noble thoughts cannot necessarily be summoned at the last moment for a desirable outcome. Thus, it is essential to always practise thinking noble thoughts, so they become second nature and remain with the individual even at the end, when the mind is likely to get agitated. If one's desire is for release or reaching the Supreme, one must meditate on the Lord at all times. When the mind is constantly focused on Him, there can be no doubt that one will remember Him at the critical time of passing and reach Him. However, this is not easy; it is a continual struggle to focus the mind on noble thoughts and deeds, and not let the mind drift towards worldly preoccupations. Having spoken about the importance of cultivating noble thoughts and deeds, Shree Krishna is aware that this may be the escape route Arjuna is looking for and dodging the task at hand. So, He brings Arjuna back to his immediate duty—reminding him of the righteous war he must fight, which he can do as an offering to Lord Krishna and is not in conflict with the teaching received. Shree Krishna explains the way one can attain God in absolute terms.

The description of the material world is given in verses 16 to 19. Scientists are engaged in discovering the mysteries of this universe. It is a never-ending process. More than what is known to humanity is yet to be explored. The Brahman is infinite. Even the Supreme Personality of Godhead is within reach, yet beyond reach. Knowing him, we become him. When a drop merges with the ocean, it loses its identity. When we merge with Him, we become Him. Lord Brahma resides in the Satya Loka. When he surrendered unto Shree Krishna, the blessed Lord showered His divine grace upon him. Now, the span of Brahma Deva's day and night has been given. The Vedic Vigyan calculates 311 trillion and 40 billion as the lifespan of Lord Brahma. Verses 20 to 22 explain the God-realisation.

The total of our lives is reflected in our thoughts. Our mind should be focused on the Divine Lotus Feet. We have to train our senses for this last moment. Finally, I would like to recite this line, which in my opinion explains the gist of this chapter: '*Jis desh mein, jis vesh mein, parivesh mein raho, Radha Raman, Radha Raman, Radha Raman kaho* (Let our thoughts be clear, our hearts be pure and our actions be truthful! Let us practise to remember God at all times, in all situations and conditions, wherever we are)!'

SUMMARY

Verses 1–7: The seven questions asked by Arjuna, Lord Krishna's reply and instructions to remember Him at all times.

Verses 8–16: The worship of God with form and without form.

Verses 17–22: Description of Brahma Loka, the greatness of God and bhakti.

Verses 23–28: The onward passage of the yogi to the next life.

KEY QUOTES

1. The Bhagavad Gita motivates us towards virtue.
2. We can change ourselves, not others.
3. We become as we think.
4. When we change ourselves, the world around us changes mysteriously.
5. Never blame others for our shortcomings.
6. A great man has a pure heart, clear thinking and truthful action.
7. Birth is predestined, but death can be modified by our efforts.
8. Shree Krishna wants us to become the directors of our lives, not mere spectators.
9. Bhajan and smaran become our nature.
10. When we learn the art of listening, we can control both external and internal listening.

9

Raj Vidya Raj Guhya Yoga

The Yoga of Royal Knowledge and Royal Secret

Total verses: 34

The ninth chapter of the Bhagavad Gita is particularly important, wherein Shree Krishna talks about devotion, attainment of knowledge and the ultimate nature of the Divine. He talks about Bhakti Yoga and leads Arjuna towards the ultimate knowledge. As the title suggests, it contains the topmost secret and the wisdom that leads to spiritual enlightenment. Not a smooth start. Herein, the importance of devotion, the nature of the Divine and the relation between the soul and the Supreme are discussed. It is foundational to understand the profound and transformative power of faith and devotion in attaining union with the Divine. Through this chapter, Lord Krishna dispels the moral and spiritual dilemmas plaguing Arjuna's mind.

The Shrimad Bhagavad Gita tells us:

1. The Gita presents the reality before us.
2. It is a 'master' encyclopaedia for the world.
3. It prods us into serving the Divine.
4. It is the mother of the entire human race.
5. It provides treatment for mental and physical ailments.
6. It breaks down differences and establishes harmony.
7. It strengthens our wisdom and instils vigour.
8. It cements the feeling of oneness.
9. It teaches us how to be detached while living in the world.
10. It explains the method of surrender to Shree Krishna.
11. It prods us into action and service.

We all seek solutions to our problems, and today, there is no dearth of quacks offering quick fixes for everything. It is a trap, but we realise it only after suffering through the ordeal. The general tendency is to run away from problems, but doing so can only cause them to increase. The scriptures, as well as the great saints, teach us to use obstacles as a stepping stone to both material and spiritual success. Mata Kunti states in the Bhagavatam, '*Vipadaha santu taha shashvat tatra tatra Jagadguro|Bhavato darshanam yat syad apunarbhava darshanam* (I pray that all those calamities happen again and again so that we can see you every time, and seeing you alone shall rid us from this cycle of rebirth)' (Shrimad Bhagavatam 1:8:25). A very reaffirming shloka of the Gita goes, '*Manmana bhava madbhakto maddyaji maam namaskuru* (Engage your mind in always thinking of me, becoming my devotee and offering obeisance by worshipping me)' (Gita 9:34). Mental strength is the bedrock of physical strength. Strong-willed people garner the courage to fight great physical adversities.

The Gita's profound knowledge is being taught by the Jagadguru, the eternal master. This is neither AI-generated nor copied and pasted from another source—it is the original knowledge of His creation. As we progress through the text, Shree Krishna peels away every layer of ignorance, thereby revealing his true self, culminating in the

Vishwaroopa Darshana in the eleventh chapter. Today, whether it's for admission into schools, colleges, universities or jobs, we need to pass an interview. Documents may be presented for identification, but an online or an in-person interview is always required before enrolment. Certificates are external proofs, but the interview is the 'inner view', a process of looking within, both by the self and others. Shree Krishna is examining Arjuna's mind, much like a doctor who performs an MRI, a nuclear scan or 3D/4D imaging. He reveals the image to Arjuna, explaining what is being seen and diagnosed. This process is necessary because the body, mind and intellect are not in sync with what the soul wants.

This chapter assimilates our scattered energies and directs them closer to God's realisation. A spiritual aspirant or a bhakta can synchronise all four with the Supreme Personality of Godhead. Spirituality guides us from entertainment to enlightenment, from excitement to inspiration, and from a feeling of tiredness to being energetic. Material things come with a shelf life. What is enjoyable now might not be so tomorrow. This is known as the law of diminishing returns. Medical science calls it anhedonia—a state that appears to mimic boredom but is marked by a deeper loss of motivation. To overcome this lethargy and enjoy contentment in life, we must offer everything to the Divine and then use or consume it as prasad. The idea behind this practice lies in transferring ownership to the Divine, thereby eliminating any pride in its possession. Indian culture incorporates the tenets of the scriptures in everyday life. This chapter teaches us to symbolically give away the Power of Attorney to the Almighty. Bhakti is not at all complicated. Simple folks are misled by so-called religious leaders to suit their ulterior motives. Shree Krishna says, '*Patram pushpam phallam ttoyam yemey bhaktya prayachhati* (If one offers me just a leaf or a flower or a fruit or just water with devotion, it is accepted by me delightfully)' (Gita 9:26). Can it be simpler than this? Our problem is that we get attached to anything and everything very easily, but with attachment, the joy goes away.

Anything done without thinking results in misery. It is akin to a snake who tries to gulp a huge toad, but it gets stuck. Neither does it go in nor can it be thrown out.

Seeing Arjuna's receptivity and maturity, Lord Krishna now opens up and reveals the ultimate secret and ultimate wisdom. He says:

Iddam tey guhyatam pravakshyamyan suuyavey|
Gyanam vigyansahitam yajgyatva mokshyasey ashubhaat||
(Gita 9:1)

(The Supreme Lord says, O Arjuna! Because you are dear to me, I shall now impart to you this confidential wisdom, knowing which you will be released from the miseries of worldly existence.)

On one hand, Lord Krishna declares this knowledge to be most confidential; on the other, it is being revealed to you and me. Though it is shared openly, its true purport is a secret. It is subtle and not easily understood. The qualification for the recipient is very simple. Nirmatsaraanam sattam is devoid of jealousy. Lord Krishna clarifies in the next shloka:

Rajvidya Rajguhyam pavitramidauttamam|
Pratyakshavagamam dharmyam susukham kartuvyayam||
(Gita 9:2)

(This knowledge is the ultimate of all sciences and the most profound of all secrets. It purifies those who listen. It is directly realisable according to dharma, easy to practise and has an everlasting effect.)

Ashraddhanah purusha dharmasyaasya Parantapa|
Aprrapya maam nivartanttey mrityusansarvartmani||
(Gita 9:3)

(People who have no faith in dharma are unable to attain me. They are stuck in this cycle of life and death.)

The Haribhaktivilas says that the first step of bhakti is faith. The beginning of Ramcharitmanas states, '*Bhavani Shankarau vanddey shraddha vishwas roopinau* (Mata Bhavani is the embodiment of faith and Lord Shiva embodies confidence or trust). Verses 10 to 14 define the divine opulence. Verses 26 and 34 address the graceful beauty of divinity or 'madhurya'. Man is bestowed with infinite possibilities, but because of ignorance, they remain unexplored. Lord Krishna says:

Mayyadhyakshena prakritihi suyattey sacharaacharam|
Hetunaanena Kaunteya jagadviparivartattey||
(Gita 9:10)

(Working under my directions, nature creates all beings, O son of Kunti! This is the cause of creation, sustenance and dissolution.)

The Lord explains the endless cycle of life. He further adds:

Avajananti maam moodha maanushim tanumaashrittam|
Param bhavamajaananto muma bhootmaheshwaram||
(Gita 9:11)

(The ignorant are unable to recognise me when I take an avatar. They do not know my divinity as the Supreme Personality of Godhead.)

Shree Krishna explains a fool or an ignorant person in the next verse.

Moghasha moghakarmanno moghagyana vichetsaha|
Raakshasi aasurrim chaiva prakritim mohinnim shritaha||
(Gita 9:12)

(Being of a deceitful nature of fiends and demons, they cherish vain hopes, perform vain actions, pursue vain knowledge and are devoid of judgement.)

In the thirteenth verse, Shree Krishna says that his devotee recognises him as immutable and the origin of all beings. The devotee is endowed with a divine nature and worships the Lord with a focused mind.

> *Satattam keertayanttomaam yattantascha dridhavrattaha|*
> *Namasyanttascha maam bhaktya nityayukta upaasattey||*
> (Gita 9:14)

(Ever glorifying me, striving with self-control, with a firm resolve, bowing before me, they worship me with love and a firm faith)

Verse 15 states that one can attain the lord through three different ways: '*Ekattvena prithakttvena bahudha vishwattomukham* (Some perceive me as undifferentiated oneness not distinct from them, while others perceive me as distinct from them. The third type worship me as the cosmic being through my endless incarnations).' He goes on to say:

> *Ttey ttam bhuktva vishaalam, ksheeney punnye martyalokam vishanti|*
> *Evam trayidharma manuprapanna, gatagattam kamakaama labhanttey||*
> (Gita 9:21)

(They, having enjoyed the pleasures of heaven, when their punya is exhausted, return to the material world. Thus, those desirous of pleasures come and go from the material world endlessly.)

Now, we have reached a famous and crucial shloka:

> *Anannyaschintayanttomaam yejanaha paryupaasattey|*
> *Tteysham nityayukttannam yogakshemam vahhamyaham||*
> (Gita 9:22)

(Those who worship me alone, thinking of no other, for those ever-united, I secure what they already possess and take care of all their needs.)

This shloka appears in the middle of this chapter, and in a way, is also at the centre of the complete text. Out of 700 verses, this is the 360th. It exemplifies the essence of the chapter, which unveils the secret of self-realisation. When we surrender unconditionally to the will of God, he takes over the responsibility for the well-being of the surrendered devotee. This is what bhakti is all about, and the great bhaktas like Meera Bai, Narsinh Mehta, Tukaram, Namdev, Janabai and Tulsi are living testaments to the truth of this shloka. Here, the Supreme Personality of Godhead is, in effect, signing a bond and declaring that he takes full responsibility for his devotee's welfare!

The various avatars of Lord Krishna only underscore this point. In the eleventh verse of the fourth chapter, Shree Krishna says, '*Ye yatha maam prapaddyanttey ttam sthathaiva bhajamyaham* (In whatever way one surrenders unto me, I reciprocate accordingly)' (Gita 4:11). The word 'ananya' is vital. In the Ramcharitmanas, Lord Rama tells Shree Hanuman, '*Sevak Priya ananyagati sou ... So ananya jakey asi matin a tarrai Hanumant| Mein sevak sacharachara roopa swami Bhagwant* (The devotee who is solely dependent on me is very dear to me ... Hanuman, the one solely dependent on me is steadfast in his conviction that he is the servant and the lord is the master of the entire creation) (*Manas, Kishkindhakanda* 3).

In the twenty-third and the twenty-fourth verses, Lord Krishna talks about the Sakama Bhakta or the devotees with desire. It says, '*Na tu maamabhijaananti tattvey natashchyavantittey* (Those who do not understand my divine nature are reborn)' (Gita 9:24). Lord Krishna says that his nature is very simple, and one does not need to perform lengthy rituals to worship him. From verses 26 to 34, Shree Krishna talks about pure madhurya bhakti, the devotion inspired by intimacy with Shree Krishna. One of the famous shlokas of the Gita is:

Patram pushpam phallam ttoyam, yomay bhaktya prayachhati|
Tadaham bhaktyuphritamashnami prayataatmanaha||
(Gita 9:26)

(If one offers me with devotion only a leaf or a flower or a fruit or even some water, I delightfully accept it.)

This stands in stark contrast to what we observe in the world. Usually, the larger the gift, the happier the receiver. Here, feeling is immaterial. But in the spiritual sphere, the object is immaterial. What is of utmost importance is the feeling behind it. Our scriptures are filled with innumerable examples of this, like the berries of Mata Shabari, the vegetable peel offered by Vidurani, the lotus plucked by Gajendra and so on. Whatever we might have done, are doing and will do, let us offer everything to the Almighty.

Yatkaroshi yadashnasi yajjuhoshi dadasi yatt|
Yattapasyasi Kaunteya, tadkurushva madarpannam||
(Gita 9:27)

(Whatever you do, whatever you eat, whatever you offer as oblations in the yagya, whatever you give as a gift and whatever austerities you perform, O son of Kunti, do it as an offering to me.)

The Gita tells us to maintain balance and equality in life. We need to inculcate intimacy with Lord Krishna into our very being and devote everything to him. It sounds very easy, but it needs diligent practice: 'Ye bhajanti tu maam bhaktya mayi ttey teshu chaapyaham (The devotee who worships me with love resides in me, and I reside in them)' (Gita 9:29). On one hand, Lord Krishna says that He is neutral and does not favour anyone. Yet, He becomes partial towards his devotees. The Almighty does not scrutinise the ones who come to him; He accepts one and all unconditionally. It is proved in this shloka:

Api chetsu duraacharo bhajatey maamnatyabhaak|
Sadhureva sa mantavyaha samyag vyavasito hi saha||
(Gita 9:30)

(Even if the vilest sinner worships me with devotion, I consider him to be righteous because he is coming to me.)

As such, every word of this text is profound, but this chapter contains some of the highest truths revealed by Lord Krishna. Any explanation of this chapter will be incomplete if we don't mention the last verse:

Manmana bhava maddbhakto maddyaji maam namaskuru|
Mameyvaishyasi yuktavaiva maatmanam mattparaayanaha||
(Gita 9:34)

(Always think of me, be my devotee, worship me and offer
obeisance to me. Having dedicated your mind and body to me,
you will certainly attain me.)

The sixty-sixth verse of the eighteenth chapter concludes this very thought. It is the culmination of the discourse wherein Lord Krishna exhorts Arjuna to just surrender unto Him without fear, and He promises to remove all his sins. Can darkness remain in light? In front of the Divine flow of grace, what is the might of a tiny sin? It is just like a tiny straw flowing away in the mighty Ganges!

In conclusion, the path to liberation lies in performing all our daily activities as an offering to the lord as a yagya. In this age of Kali, Shree Chaitanya Mahaprabhu has shown us the most inclusive and accessible path: chant the divine name of the lord. Hari Naam Sankirtana is the essence of bhakti. Let us offer all that we do and the fruits of our karmas at the Divine Lotus Feet. Unconditional devotion is the 'Raj Path' to the Divine. Every action should be performed with dedication, as a service to the lord. Raja Yoga is the combination of Karma Yoga and Bhakti Yoga. On this path, even our kama and krodha are offered to God. The cows symbolise our senses, lost in this forest of the world: *Tum dhoondo mujhey, Gopal, main tori gaiya bhooli si* (Hey, Krishna! You being the cowherd, please call them to you)!'

SUMMARY

Verses 1–2:	The glory of this secret wisdom.
Verses 3–4:	The envious, devoid of faith, will not be able to understand it.
Verses 5–10:	The explanation of the essence of Divine majesty.
Verses 11–12:	The definition of a fool.
Verses 13–14:	The qualities of the bhakta and the nature of a mahatma.
Verse 15:	The three paths leading to God.
Verses 16–21:	The Virat Swaroopa and the actions prescribed by the Vedas.
Verse 22:	The complete responsibility of his devotee.
Verses 23–24:	The definition of a Sakama Bhakta.
Verses 25–34:	Exposition of Madhurya Bhakti.

KEY QUOTES

1. To love God and to ask something from Him are two separate things.
2. The establishment of equanimity is the essence of the Gita.
3. Do not be a competitor; become a partner.
4. Spirituality does not tire you; it motivates you.
5. Do not get attached to anything; offer it to the Divine.
6. We must direct our body, mind, intellect and the soul in one direction.
7. We need to explore the infinite possibilities that exist within us.
8. Whatever we offer can be limited, but our feelings should be infinite.
9. We need to mould our mind, body, intellect and soul to bow down and follow the right path.

10

Vibhuti Yoga

The Yoga of Divine Manifestations

Total verses: 42

Let us imagine the progressive blossoming of a lotus. The process begins with the first rays of the sun, leading to the complete blooming of the flower. Similarly, here Shree Krishna is the sun, and His words are the rays of sunlight which open the lotus of Arjuna's heart. In the first chapter, Arjuna descends into deep despondency, akin to the muck where the lotus grows. From there, the evolutionary process begins as the lotus raises its head out of the waters. Over the past nine chapters, Lord Krishna was showing Arjuna the inner world, explaining the 'power within' that keeps us all alive. The Divine dwells equally in all beings, without distinction. This is the secret of 'Para Brahman' as unveiled in the last chapter. Now, the outer world is being revealed. 'Vibhuti' literally means the sacred ash. To understand it better, let's split the word into 'vibhu' and 'bhuti'. 'Vibhu' means omnipresent, and 'bhuti' means thriving or existence.

'Vibhuti' has many meanings, including glory or all-pervading or abundant or presiding over. This chapter explores the glories of the Supreme Personality of Godhead; therefore, it is called Vibhuti Yoga. To truly experience the Divine presence, we need to understand the intrinsic nature of the Divine—that is, the means to see Him everywhere, in everything and in all situations. This means that the impulses brought in by the senses must be examined through the intellect, using the faculty of reasoning. Recognising divinity in all helps us to respond correctly.

Lord Shiva, who is often seen smeared in ash, is a powerful symbol. Anything when burnt turns into ash. Before being burnt, it had a name, form and qualities attached to it. It had its individuality. When burnt, it loses all such traits. Name, form and qualities are indirectly responsible for the ego's development, which often leads to arrogance and, fuelled by lust and anger, becomes violent. When burnt, all this turns into ash, which Lord Shiva smears all over because there is no trace of ego in it. Another way of looking at it is that the first nine chapters represent Navadha Bhakti, each signifying one aspect culminating into Divine love. The tenth chapter of the Gita and the Dasham Skandha (tenth Canto) of Shrimad Bhagavatam reveal the true nature of the Divine. To comprehend this chapter, the last verse of the ninth chapter is very significant. It says:

Manmana bhava madbhakto maddyaji maama namaskuru|
Maameyvaishyasi yuktavaivam atmanam matparaayannah||
(Gita 9:34)

(Fix your mind on me, be devoted to me, surrender unto me and bow down to me. Having thus disciplined yourself, regarding me as the ultimate goal, you will attain me.)

Unless we unconditionally surrender unto Him, we cannot attain Him. As long as we identify with the body, mind and the intellect, we connect the material world and experience pleasure and pain. The moment we relate to the atman, we transcend the material world and enter the realm of eternal bliss. In today's world, educational qualifications matter, while spiritual qualifications are often overlooked. The study of the Gita qualifies us spiritually and intellectually. It is both theory and practice. Shree Krishna first imparted the theory, and now he is guiding Arjuna to experience it, allowing it to become deeply ingrained in his psyche. The moment we embrace spirituality, our entire outlook changes. 'ME' becomes 'WE'! Man has immense possibilities. Spirituality transforms a dacoit into a sage, '*Balmiki bhaye Brahma samaana* (Dacoit Valmiki became Divine).' The Gita starts with negation and is transformed, in the eighteenth chapter, into affirmation: 'I will do as you say.' Lord Krishna instilled self-discipline in Arjuna, along with giving him complete liberty to choose what he wants. 'Every action has an equal and an opposite reaction' is Newton's third law of motion. If anything is done by force, it will eventually revolt or prove ineffective. Kama in itself is not so bad as much as the constant thought of it. The Gita converts our 'vishaad' into 'prasad'! Arjuna says:

Nashtto mohah smritirlabdha tvatprasadan mayyachyuta|
Sthittosmi gatasandehah karishye vachannam tava||
(Gita 18:73)

(Arjuna says: 'My delusion has been destroyed and I have regained my memory through your Divine grace, O Krishna! I now stand firm, free from doubt and will do as you say.')

The Bhagavad Gita teaches self-discipline. On the one hand, it emphasises self-discipline; on the other, it upholds the complete freedom of action. In my view, this is the bedrock of democracy. This sutra is elaborated in the Kathopanishad. The familiar image of Shree Krishna and Arjuna seated on the chariot, with the Lord holding the reins in his hand, is instantly associated with the Bhagavad Gita. The five horses represent our senses; Arjuna represents each one of us;

and the reins, symbolising control over the senses, are held by the Supreme Lord.

This is the essence of this eternal text. Unless this is done, our life will be topsy-turvy, and the chances of a mishap become very high. Enjoyment of the senses is not an issue, but it becomes problematic because of obsessive preoccupation. By shifting our mindset from 'impossible' to 'I'm possible', we move from the negative to the positive. As the last chapter concludes, Lord Krishna advises: keep the mind attached or devoted or focused on me at all times. In response, Arjuna asks the Lord: since he doesn't fully know the Supreme, how can he focus his mind on Him? This is the central theme of the chapter. Shree Krishna reveals his divinity to Arjuna, enabling him to completely surrender to the Ultimate Reality, that is, Shree Krishna himself. The practice of perceiving the Divine in a very wide spectrum helps us realise our own smallness in contrast to the Lord Krishna's vast, all-pervasive presence. Lord Krishna says that the peepul, or the bodhi tree or the sacred fig, is His vibhuti. Amongst the various yagynas, He is the Japa Yagna. Amongst the sense organs or the indriyas, He is the mind. Through a few illustrations, He reveals His Divinity, saying that He is everything, seen or unseen. This leads us to the core of the Bhagavad Gita, the Shree Vijay.

Yatra Yogeshwaraha Krishno yatra Partho dhanurdharaha|
Tatra Shree Vijayobhuti dhruva neetir matirmama ||
(Gita 18:78)

(Wherever Yogeshwar Lord Krishna and his devotee Partha are there, victory, prosperity, righteousness and happiness abide.)

Comprehending the vibhuti or the Divine glory or magnificence leads us to the supreme realisation. The gopis of Shree Dham Vrindavan experience Shree Krishna in this very way: '*Iti Kishoriji-tasya anubhoota tasya ashritaha* (The handmaids of Shree Kishori Ji experience Shree Krishna through her in the same way).'

Bhakti has four elements: '*Bhakti, bhakta, bhagwanta, guru chaturnaam vapu ek* (Bhakti, the devotee, the lord, and the sadguru are the four different identities of the same reality).' The eighth chapter spoke about the bhakta, the ninth addressed bhakti, and now we come to the tenth, revealing Bhagwan or the Supreme Personality of Godhead: '*Yam Brahma samupaasattey Shiva iti Brahmeti vedantino, Baudhaha Buddhaiti pramaanaha patthavaha karteti naiyayika* (The Supreme is beyond comprehension even for Brahma and Lord Shiva).' Even the vedantins or the logicians following the Nyaya philosophy cannot comprehend Him. One who is beyond comprehension says, '*Aham bhakta paradheeno* (I am subservient to my devotees).' The Shrimad Bhagavatam says, '*Durlabho maanushu deho deheenam kshanabhanguraha, tatraadi durlabham mannye Vaikunthapriya darshanam* (Precious is this human body, though perishable, but those who love the Lord of Vaikuntha or His dear devotees are invaluable)' (Shrimad Bhagavatam 11.2.29).

Lord Krishna makes himself easily accessible, but it is here that the greatness of his devotee comes to the forefront. Through his benevolence, Lord Krishna leads us to a saint, and the saint, out of his deep compassion, leads us to God. It is as if each is intent on glorifying the other. The Padma Purana defines the Supreme, saying: '*Uttpatti pralayam chaiva bhootanam agati gati|Venti vidyaam avidyaam cha sa vaachyo Bhagawaniti* (The scriptures define Shree Bhagwan as the one who has these six qualities, Aishwarya or glory, Dharma, Yasha or fame, Shree or magnificence, wisdom and dispasion). If we try to decipher the word 'Bhagwan' further, 'bha' is earth, 'ga' is the sky, 'wa' is air and 'n' is water. Shree Krishna is the Divine incarnate. Out of His infinite grace, He has gifted humanity the divine nectar in the form of the Gita.

Sarvopanishado gavo dogdha Gopalnandanaha|
Partho vatsaha sudhirbhokta dugddham Geetamrittam mahat||
(Gita Mahatmya 6)

(All the Upanishads are the cows, the son of the cowherd, Gopal, that is, Shree Krishna, is the milkman, and Partha is the calf. The men of purified intellect are the drinkers of this divine nectar in the form of the Gita.)

A realised soul reflects upon the Divine in different ways. In the first chapter, Lord Krishna is quiet, whereas Arjuna goes on and on. Here, He is so eager to reveal Himself that He does not wait for Arjuna's queries. Here, Lord Krishna openly expresses his love for his devotee and says:

Bhooya aeva mahabaho shrinnu mmey paramam vachaha|
Yatteyhampriyamaannaya vakshyami hitakaamyaya||
(Gita 10:1)

(The Lord says, O mighty armed, now attentively listen to me for I want to reveal to you my eternal truth as you are dear to me and I seek your ultimate welfare.)

In this verse, Lord Krishna uses four exhortations: mighty armed, my dear, supreme word and ultimate welfare. It shows the outpouring of Lord Krishna's divine love for his dear devotee, just like a mother's love for her child.

Na mey viduhu surganaha prabhavam na maharshayaha|
Ahamadirhi Devanaam maharshinnam cha sarvashaha||
(Gita 10:2)

(Neither the heavenly beings nor the great sages know my origin, for I am the very source)

Yo maamajam aaddim cha vetti lokamaheshwaram|
Asammuddhaha sa martyeshu sarva paapaihi pramuchyattey||
(Gita 10:3)

(He who knows me as the unborn, as the beginningless, as the Supreme Lord of all existence, only such an undeluded person is freed from all sins.)

Here, Lord Krishna indicates the partial effect of the Vibhuti Yoga. Starting from the fourth verse till the seventh, he describes various feelings and situations—in short, everything that exists or doesn't exist is He.

> *Aettam vibhooti yogam cha mumma yo vetti tattvataha|*
> *So avikampena yogena yujyattey naatra sanshayaha||*
> (Gita 10:7)

(The one who completely understands and is convinced of this opulence and my mystic prowess engages in unalloyed devotional service unto me, without any doubt.)

To know is one thing, but to surrender is something entirely different. Knowledge may come easily, but surrendering unconditionally is very difficult. Yet, after gaining true understanding, Arjuna completely surrenders himself at the Lotus Feet of Shree Krishna. Verses 8 to 11 of this chapter are important. The great acharyas have declared these shlokas to be the very essence of the Gita. They can be regarded as a condensed summary of all 700 shlokas.

> *Aham sarvasya Prabhavo mattaha sarvam pravartattey|*
> *Iti matva bhajanttey maam budha bhaavasamanvitaha||*
> (Gita 10:8)

(I am the source of the spiritual and the material worlds. Everything emanates from me. The ones who know this perfectly engage in my devotional service and worship me with all their hearts.)

In the Madhya Leela of Shree Chaitanya Charita-Amrita, this sentiment is expressed:

> *Bhagwan sambandha, bhakti abhidheya hoya|*
> *Prema prayojana vedey teen vastu koya||*

(The Vedic literatures declare the jeeva's relationship with Shree Krishna, known as 'sambandha'. Understanding it and acting accordingly is called 'abhidheya'. Returning home to God is the ultimate goal, known as 'prayojana'.)

The eighth verse is the essence, the ninth is the relationship with Shree Krishna, the tenth is the Bhakti Abhidheya, and the eleventh is Prema Prayojana.

Dharmaha projjhittaika tavo atra paramo Nirmatasaraanam sattam vedyam vaastavamatra vastu Shivaddam taapatrayon moolannam
(Bhagwat 1:1:2)

(Completely rejecting all materially motivated religious activities, this text espouses the highest truth, which is understood by only the pure-hearted souls. The ultimate truth is for the welfare of one and all, and it destroys all the miseries.)

*Matchitta maddgatapranna bodhayantaha parasparam|
Kathayanttashcha maama nityam tushyantti cha ramantti cha||*
(Gita 10:9)

(With the mind wholly resting in me, with the senses absorbed in me, enlightening one another and forever speaking of me, they are contented and delighted.)

The relationship with the Divine and the ultimate goal may be easily understood, but the process and the essence of that journey can only be realised through the benevolent grace of the sadguru. I stress the importance of these four for a simple reason: they reveal the process of comprehending the ultimate truth. In these shlokas, Lord Krishna himself explains the process of attaining Him.

*Tteyshaam satat uktannam bhajattam preeti purvakam|
Daddami buddhiyoggam ttam yena maamupayantittey||*
(Gita 10:10)

(To the ever steadfast, worshipping me with love, I grant the Buddhi Yoga to them through which they come to me.)

Teyshamayva anukampartha mahamagyaanjjam tamaha|
Naashayaamyatmbhaavastho gyandeepena bhaasvata||
(Gita 10:11)

(Hey Arjuna! Out of compassion, I dwell within their hearts and destroy the darkness born out of ignorance by lighting the luminous lamp of knowledge.)

Param Brahmah param dhaama pavittram paramam bhavaan|
Purusham shaashwattam divyam aadideva majjam vibhum||
(Gita 10:12)

(Arjuna says, 'You are the Supreme Brahman, the supreme abode, the supreme purifier, eternal, the Supreme Personality of Godhead, the God of all Gods, unborn and omnipresent.')

Arjuna is now inching towards knowing the Supreme, yet I feel that he asks this question for our benefit. Like we see in the Shrimad Bhagwat, Shree Shukadeva Ji Maharaj appreciates the question asked by Shree Parikshit and says:

Vareeyanesha ttey prashnaha krato lokahittam nripa|
Atmavitt sammataha punnsam shrotavyadishu yaha paraha||
(Bhagwat 2:1:1)

(O mighty king! You have asked a very pertinent question for the general good of mankind, which will be instrumental in their liberation.)

From the twelfth to the eighteenth verse, Arjuna sings the glories of Lord Krishna and is eager to go on listening without end.

Vistareynnaatmano yogam vibhoottim cha Janardana|
Bhooyaha kathaya traptirhi shrunnvatto naasti mey amrittam||
(Gita 10:18)

(Please go on speaking, my lord, as now my thirst for this divine nectar is multiplying manifold.)

This thought is even reflected in the Shrimad Bhagwat: '*Leelamrita rasonmatraha katha maatraika jeevinaha| Harihi sharannamevam hee nityam yesham mukhey vachaha* (The one who tastes this nectar of Shree Hari Katha even once gets addicted to it in such a way that he cannot stay without it even for a moment) (Bhagwat Mahatmya 47). From verses 19 to 42, Shree Krishna narrates eighty-two glories and manifestations to Arjuna in short, for He is 'Ananta', beyond comprehension, yet is making himself easily accessible for you and me. Lord Krishna further added:

Ahamatma Guddakesha sarvabhoota shayasthitaha|
Ahamaadishcha madhyam cha bhootanaamanta eva cha||
(Gita 10:20)

(I am the atman, O Arjuna, seated in the hearts of all the creatures. I am the beginning, the middle and the end of all beings.)

Briefly, He declares: 'I am Vishnu, I am the Sun, the Moon, Samaveda, Agni, Kubera, Sumeru and so on.' Shree Krishna encompasses the whole of creation, giving a glimpse of the outer form while revealing the ultimate reality: He is omnipresent and omniscient. The Bhagavad Gita presents this vision in its proper place and perspective. It is rooted in the recognition of the Divine self within all beings, both eminent and obscure. God must be seen and loved in the ignorant, the humble, the weak, the vile, the outcast. While we may be a higher manifestation of nature compared to animals, Brahman abides equally in all. Shree Krishna tells us that He is the master of the universe and the origin of this creation. He expresses himself in nature as the soul of every living entity, asking us to see and experience His omnipresence. This is the basic purport of this chapter.

SUMMARY

Verses 1–7:	The description of Vibhuti Yoga and its glories.
Verses 8–11:	The description of Bhagavad Bhakti and Bhagavad Kripa.
Verses 12–18:	Arjuna's prayer.
Verses 19–42:	The description of Lord Krishna's magnificence or vibhutis.

KEY QUOTES

1. The Bhagavad Gita alters our outlook towards life.
2. The Gita starts with inability but ends with stability.
3. The Gita teaches us self-discipline along with granting complete freedom.
4. The gratification of the senses isn't as bad as constantly thinking about it.
5. The 'darshan' of the Lord is not so difficult, but to be able to see or meet his dear devotee is very difficult.
6. Prema does not lead us from the question to the answer; instead, it leads us into a state of maun or complete silence.
7. The God-realised soul becomes Godlike!
8. Only the beloved can understand the indication.
9. Emotions don't interfere in the realm of prema.
10. Acquiring knowledge is simple, but surrendering unconditionally is very difficult.

11

Vishwa Roopa Darshan Yoga

The Yoga of the Vision of the Universal Cosmic Form

Total verses: 55

The Bhagavad Gita describes the true nature of the human soul, considered one with the Divine spirit that animates all of creation. Previously, Shree Krishna stated how his presence permeates everything, showing that the self underlies the manifold forms of existence. These various manifestations point to the self as the substratum of this diverse world. In other words, the atman is a part of the paramatman and pervades in the entire creation. Now, Lord Krishna shows Arjuna that everything exists within the self. It is easier to see the self in finite objects than to comprehend the entire universe as a single, unified reality rooted in the self.

The concept of space divides individual objects from one another. If there is no space in between, all objects will come together and merge into a single entity. In this unified mass of things, there will be different shapes and forms in the same place at the same time. This is the picturisation of the Universal or the Cosmic Being, the vision of the world in a mind which has gone beyond the concept of space and time.

Shree Krishna removes this limited perception from Arjuna's mind and assumes his universal form, proving that everything in the universe exists within Him. Seeing the Supreme Personality of Godhead, Arjuna is compelled to revisit his faith and understanding. Arjuna is wonderstruck, bewildered, and filled with fear, reverence, devotion—all at the same time. This chapter's concept and description are among the highest philosophical and metaphysical treatises among all the sacred texts. When approached in its true spirit, it instantly transforms us from materialism to spiritualism. Arjuna's transformation unfolds across his mental, intellectual and spiritual planes. In the first chapter, we saw Arjuna tremble out of sheer despair. Here, we see him tremble out of fear after witnessing the cosmic, ginormous form of Lord Krishna. Arjuna's outlook undergoes a momentous change. We must learn to see the good or positive in everything. Generally, people notice flaws in the most perfect things! Human life is beset with innumerable difficulties. This is true for the saint and the sinner. However, their approach differs. It calls for a different set of eyes—divya chakshu—which Arjuna is blessed with by Shree Krishna, just as new-age gadgets enable us to view things multidimensionally.

People believe that by changing the environment, the situation will also change. But it doesn't. Everyone is stuck in a rut! Each element of life can't be conducive for a person. Shree Mahaprabhu was roaming in the forests in and around Bengal, but in his heart, he was in Shree Dham Vrindavan: '*Radha kunda Shyam kunda aaro giri Govardhan, Madhur-madhur bansi baajey aei toh aamar Brindabon* (The Radha Kunda, Shyam Kunda, the Govardhan Hill, where the sweet melody of the divine flute can be heard, is my Vrindavan)' (Gaudiya Bhajan). During his conversation with Shree

Rai Ramananda, He visualised the 'Neelanchal' as Shree Braj on one end and Shree Dwarika at the other. Here, neither the place nor the situation changed—only Arjuna's outlook did. When our outlook changes, things change automatically. We look at the world according to our perception, and this varies from person to person. To enable Arjuna to see the divinity in the creation, Lord Krishna blesses him with divine eyesight. Or, I may say, insight. Goswami Tulsidas says, '*Nija mann mukura sudhaar* (I cleanse the mirror of my mind).' We need to practise seeing the good in everything. When we shout, the Almighty may or may not hear. But when the words escape the depths of our hearts, they are surely heard by Him. When the gopi speaks, her words are heard by Shree Krishna because, '*Vaikhari varna roopa iti mati*', and finally culminating into: '*Iti gopyaha pragaayantyaha pralappantyashcha chitradha, ruruduhu suswaram Rajan Krishna darshan laalsaha* (Shree Shukadeva Ji tells Shree Parikshit that the gopis thus went on singing, speaking deliriously and weeping endearingly for the audience of their beloved Krishna).'

In a way, the tenth chapter is an aural presentation of Shree Krishna's swaroopa. But this chapter presents His visual form, only seen through the insight given by the Divine Himself. In the previous chapter, Lord Krishna equated Arjuna with himself—Paandavannam Dhananjaya: I am you. However, Arjuna, who is undergoing the process of self-realisation, finally surrenders unto him, turning into His true devotee. This is a universal process, not specific to any particular religion. Shree Krishna represents the Almighty or the Ultimate Truth. Arjuna represents you and me, that is, humanity. Great personalities, avatars, prophets or saints speak the universal language. People often try to mould words to suit themselves. While words have many interpretations, the purport can only be explained by the master or the preceptor. One explains it as it is, without distortion or personal projection. Lord Krishna is virat or cosmic as well as swarat, meaning self-ruling or independent.

It carries a strong, empowering connotation, reflecting a sense of personal strength.

The tenth and the eleventh chapters are intertwined. The tenth says, 'me in all', whereas the eleventh is 'all in me'. Nature is an integral part of our lives. It is always evolving, but we don't notice these subtle changes unless there is a natural calamity. Upon seeing that Arjuna's perception is aligning with the Ultimate Reality, Shree Krishna blesses him with a divine vision. Now, his devotee can see beyond time and space. The James Webb telescope can only see what is within this creation, but not beyond. The vision granted by Lord Krishna to Arjuna was multidimensional and beyond any boundaries of space and time. He saw the creation, preservation and annihilation happening in one frame. We say that the human mind has unlimited possibilities; however, this too has certain limitations. But here Shree Krishna first shows Arjuna the ananda swaroopa, then the form of His creation, followed by the picturisation of time or kala, and ultimately pralaya, cataclysm or annihilation. Basically, we have to study all three stages of creation, preservation and destruction to realise the Ultimate Reality. Though scary, it is the essential truth we need to understand. When we assimilate this truth in our lives, our view of looking at the world and all that abides in it automatically changes, or, if I may say, becomes realistic.

From verses 1–8, Arjuna is praying while Lord Krishna is preparing him for the divine vision. The first four verses are Arjuna's humble submission.

Madanugrahaya paramam guhyam adhyatmasangyittam|
Yatvayoktam vachastteyna mohoyam vigato mumma||
(Gita 11:1)

(Arjuna says, 'My Lord, out of your sheer compassion, you have revealed your innermost self and taught me the confidential spiritual secrets. My illusion has been dispelled.')

Bhavapyayao he bhootanam shruttau vistarasho muya|
Tvattaha kamalpatraaksha mahaatmyapi chaavyayam||
(Gita 11:2)

(O Lotus-eyed Lord! I have heard in detail the appearance and disappearance of all living entities and have had a glimpse of your inexhaustible glories.)

Evameyttadyathaatha tvamaatmanam Parameshwara|
Drashttumichhaami ttey Roopam Aeshwaram Purushottama||
(Gita 11:3)

(O Almighty! Though I see you here in front of me, I wish to see your cosmic manifestation as described by you.)

Manyasey yadi ttachhakyam muya drashttumiti Prabho|
Yogeshwar tatto mey tvam darshayaatmaanam avyayam||
(Gita 11:4)

(If you think that I can behold your cosmic form, my Lord, then kindly reveal to me your universal self.)

Though Shree Krishna addresses Arjuna as a dear friend, we see the humility in his submission towards his master. Humility is the sadhu's foremost virtue. Along with simplicity and respect for others, it is the hallmark of one's nobility. Our scriptures say, '*Vidya dadaati vinayam*,' or knowledge makes one humble. But the world doesn't uphold this belief. As the sermon of the Gita progresses, Arjuna's knowledge rises, but its expression is the eradication of his ignorance. These verses reflect Arjuna's humility. Initially, a devotee moving on the path of bhakti doubts his capabilities, his devotion, the mantra, his guru and even the existence of God. Being humble is not a sign of weakness; it stems from a position of strength. This strength is of the Divine, not the devotee. Lord Krishna empowers bhakti, and in turn, the bhakta gets empowered.

On hearing the humble words of His devotee, Lord Krishna says:

Pashya mey Partha roopanni shatshoatha sahasrashaha|
Nanavidhani divyaani nanavarnnakriteeni cha||
(Gita 11:5)

(The Blessed Lord says, Behold, O Partha, my divine forms.)

In the eighth verse, Lord Krishna says that I now give you that divine vision or insight to behold my Universal Cosmic form. Very few individuals are blessed with this gift. Mahatma Vidura could see this form when Lord Krishna went as an ambassador of peace to Hastinapur before the Mahabharata war. During Shree Krishna's childhood, Mata Yashoda got a glimpse of this vision in his mouth. This divine vision is also obtained in Prema Bhakti when '*Akuto bhaye bhayam naasti* (My bhakta becomes fearless)'. From verses 9 to 12, Sanjaya describes to Dhritarashtra the transformation in the form of Shree Krishna. In the twelfth verse, he says, '*Divi suryasahastrasya bhaveydyuga padduthita* (If the splendour of a thousand Suns was to blaze simultaneously)' (Gita 11:12). The divine splendour is inexplicable, but from verses 15 to 31, Arjuna, utterly amazed, expresses whatever little he could comprehend.

Pashyami Devanstava Deva dehey, sarvaanstatha
bhootvisheshsanghaan|
Brahmaanmeesham Kamalaasanastha, mrusheenshcha
sarvaanuragaanshcha divyaan||
(Gita 11:15)

(Arjuna says, 'I see all the gods, O Supreme, in your body and hosts of various classes of beings. Brahma, the Lord of Creation, seated on the Lotus, all the rishis, Naga Devata and the celestial beings.')

Verses 9 to 31 portray the universality or the unfathomable swaroopa of the Supreme. Verses 9 to 14 are spoken by Sanjaya, and 15 to 31 by Arjuna. Sanjaya was blessed with divine vision by the grace of Shree Vyasa Deva, whereas Arjuna was blessed by Lord Krishna Himself. Shree Vyasa Narayan is also one of the twenty-four avatars of the Supreme.

Drishtakaraalani cha ttey mukhani, drishtaiva kaalaanlasannibhani|
Dishon a jaaney na labhey cha sharma, praseeda Devesha Jagganiwasa||
(Gita 11:25)

(Seeing your fearsome blazing mouths spewing pralaya agni, I cannot see the different directions nor do I find peace, my Lord, please be gracious, O Lord of the Devas, O Abode of the Universe.)

Arjuna witnesses the ferocious form of Kala in Shree Krishna. From verses 26 to 30, the Lord shows Kurukshetra in totality, where the Mahabharata war is being fought. Astonished and wonderstruck, Arjuna in the thirty-first verse asks Lord Krishna, 'Please tell me who are you.'

Aakhyahi mey ko bhavanugraroopo, namostu ttey Devavara praseeda|
Vigyatumichhami bhavantmaaddyam, na he prajaanami tava pravittim||
(Gita 11:31)

(Please tell me who you are, O ferocious one? I bow down and salute you, O Supreme Lord! Please have mercy on me! I desire to know you, the primordial Supreme, though I do not know your purpose.)

In the previous verse, Arjuna addresses Him as 'Pratapanti Vishno', and now he is asking Him, who are you? In verses 32 to 34, Lord Krishna clarifies that He is 'Mahakala', the destroyer who is devouring everyone and everything He has created. He says, whether you fight or you don't, all those whom you see arraigned here, ready to fight, are already in the jaws of death. Therefore, *'Nimittamatram bhava Savyasachin* (You are just an instrument, and be sure, I shall do the rest!)' (Gita 11:33). On one hand, Shree Krishna is assuring Arjuna that He will take care of everything, but the word He is using to address Arjuna is 'Savyasachin', a great warrior adept at using his weapons with both hands. Whatever we do in life, we must try to do it to the best of our capabilities. Only then can we achieve greatness. Shree Krishna asks Arjuna to perform his duty with complete trust in Him, for He shall accomplish all that needs to be accomplished.

Dronnam cha Bhishmam cha Jayadratham cha Karnam tatha anyanapi yodhaveerann|
Muya hattanstava jahi ma vyathishtha yudhyasva jetasi ranney sapattnann||
(Gita 11:34)

(Drona, Bheeshma, Jayadratha, Karna and all the other warriors have already been slain by me, and you will kill them in the battlefield. So, do not be distressed, go ahead and fight for you shall conquer your enemies, I assure you.)

Aettachhutva vachanam Keshavasya krttanjalirvepamaanaha keeritti|
Namaskritva bhooya evaaha Krishnam sakadgaddam bheetbheetaha prannamya||
(Gita 11:35)

(Sanjaya says, 'Having heard the reassuring words of Shree Keshava, Arjuna, with folded hands, trembling with fear, prostrating, bowing down, spoke in choked voice, overwhelmed with fear.')

From verses 36 to 46, Arjuna is praying and begging for pardon again and again. Arjuna is Shree Krishna's dear friend, yet is seeking the Lord's pardon, while in Shree Braj, Shree Krishna's friends consider Him to be their equal and share a natural, loving affection towards Him. These are two different categories of friendship.

Kireettinam gaddinam chakrahasttam ichhami ttvam drashtumaham tathaiva|
Tteynaiva roopena Chaturbhujena Sahasrabaaho bhava Vishwamoortey||
(Gita 11:46)

(I pray to see your four-armed form, my Lord, wearing your bejewelled crown, holding the mace and chakra in your hands. I behold your universal form, O thousand-armed Lord.)

Ittyarjunnam Vasudevastathoktva swakkam Roopam darshayamaas bhooyaha|
Aashvaasyamaas cha bheetmeynam bhootva punaha saumyavapurmahatma||
(Gita 11:50)

(Sanjaya says, 'Having thus spoken to Arjuna, Shree Vaasudeva showed the four-armed form and very gently consoled the terrified Arjuna.)

Drishtavedam maanusham Roopam tava saumyam Janardana|
Idaanimasmi sanvrattaha sachetaha prakrattim gataha||
(Gita 11:51)

(Arjuna says, 'Seeing your gentle original form, O Janardana, I am now composed and reassured.')

On seeing the virat swaroopa, Arjuna understood the secret behind life and death. All that exists does so only through divine presence. When one comprehends the omnipresence of the Supreme Reality, it becomes clear that the ordained manifestation of the Supreme Being cannot be altered and influenced by the individual turning away from the world of action because of fear and ignorance. Finally, all his misgivings about participating in the war disappear, and he is now ready to do his part. Lord Krishna further assuaged his perturbed nerves by very affectionately talking about devotion.

Verses 52 to 55 are filled with devotional fervour. So far, Shree Krishna exhibited His Universal Cosmic form, one that cannot be seen without His grace. In these verses, He speaks of the intricacies of bhakti. Shree Krishna says that this form cannot be perceived through the Vedas, austerity, knowledge or any other means. Only those who surrender to Him with complete devotion can behold Him as He now appears. Srila Roopa Goswami Pada says, '*Annyabhilashita shoonyam aanukulyena Krishnanusheelanam* (Having no desire other than surrendering unto Shree Krishna).'

Mattkarma krinmattparamo maddbhaktaha sangavarjittaha|
Nirvairaha sarvabhooteshu yaha sa maametti Pandava||
(Gita 11:55)

(The one whose actions are for me, who knows me as the Supreme, who is devoted to me, free from all attachments, harbouring no envy, comes to me only, O Pandava.)

Here, Shree Krishna briefly explains the characteristics of the devotee. In this chapter, we see the Lord in His fiercest and most affectionate form. We need to nurture humility in our hearts. Humility gives birth to compassion, culminating in a state of divine love. To do this, we don't need to go anywhere; we need to change our outlook. This chapter instils self-analysis, and by doing so, we not only purify ourselves but also start radiating purity all around.

SUMMARY

Verses 1–8:	Arjuna prays to see the Cosmic Universal form and is given the divine vision.
Verses 9–14:	Sanjaya sees the virat swaroopa.
Verses 15–31:	Arjuna sees the virat swaroopa and prays.
Verses 32–34:	Lord Krishna talks about His Cosmic form and commands Arjuna to fight.
Verses 35–46:	Arjuna surrenders in prayer.
Verses 47–50:	Shree Krishna explains His inaccessible form and reassures terrified Arjuna.
Verses 51–55:	Shree Krishna talks about the glory of His divine form and how to approach Him.

KEY QUOTES

1. See the good in everything.
2. We need to change our outlook, without changing the place.
3. Samartha or the one who is able does what he says.
4. Humility and simplicity characterise a sadhu, and we must inculcate these traits.
5. The true lover is fearless.
6. The strong one is humble, and the humble is naturally surrendered.
7. Our outlook should not be constricted; it should be universal.
8. We need to look up and within, not down and without.
9. We need to excel in whatever we do so that we can do greater things.
10. Selfishness results in pain, charity gives happiness, but any action done with a sense of worship becomes blissful.
11. The ego is the root cause of all problems.

12

Bhakti Yoga

The Yoga of Devotion

Total verses: 27

Studying the Bhagavad Gita under the able guidance of a guru, who has meditated upon and seen the text through different perspectives, enables us to understand the nuances Shree Krishna applies to impart divine knowledge to His dear disciple, Arjuna. All this while, we were being prepared for tasting the amrit, the divine nectar of bhakti. I belong to the bhakti tradition, so this is my favourite subject, and I can go on talking about it.

This chapter is most certainly the Lake of Divine Nectar. Just as a tiny drop of amrit is enough to bring the dead back to life, there are only twenty verses expounding on the tenets of devotion. Every word is a gem.

The first six chapters deal with life science and karma. From chapters six to twelve, Lord Krishna prepares us for bhakti. The sixth chapter speaks of how concentrating on the Supreme leads to surrender, the ninth chapter and the tenth chapter talk about realising the omnipresence of the Supreme, and in the eleventh chapter the ultimate reality is revealed in the form of the Vishwa-Roopa-Darshan.

There are several texts exclusively dealing with bhakti, like the Narada Bhakti Sutra and Shandilya Bhakti Sutra. Shrimad Bhagavatam also predominantly speaks about the devotion to Shree Krishna. In the present age, bhakti or devotional surrender to the Supreme Personality of Godhead can be accomplished by one and all unconditionally. In the sixth chapter, Lord Krishna emphatically declares that among all yogis, the one who has faith, always abides in Him, contemplates Him within and offers transcendental, loving service is the most intimately connected with Him in yoga, and is the highest of all (Gita 6:47).

The study of the Gita or, for that matter, any spiritual text with utmost devotion is also a service to the Divine. When the Supreme Being wants to shower His choicest of blessings upon us, He gives us His bhakti, which is a way of giving Himself to us. This is the essence of the eleventh chapter, and in the fifty-fifth verse, Shree Krishna says that the one who offers every action or karma to Him, who is unconditionally devoted, completely free of attachments, is His dearest devotee. Unencumbered devotion is the essence, and to attain it, we don't have to go anywhere; just turning our gaze inwards does the trick. Bhakti Yoga in the Gita is explained across twenty verses. Although short, it carries a deep-rooted meaning, and its explanation can be very exhaustive. Bhakti is an emotion, and for a devotee to be able to express the feelings completely at the Lotus Feet of the Beloved becomes very difficult. The Supreme Personality of Godhead, though being beyond comprehension, can still be described according to one's perception, but bhakti cannot be explained. Shree Narada in his Sutras says, anirvachaneeyam—beyond expression. In the Shrimad Bhagavatam, the gopis ultimately fall silent: *'Iti gopyaha pragaayantyaha pralappantyashcha chitradha*

(The Gopis sung, spoke and then wept for the lord, becoming still)' (Shrimad Bhagavatam 10:32:1). This is the ultimate state of divine love: when words fall short, the tears speak and reveal much more than words!

The Bhagavad Gita is an eternal text, and while the form available to all of us today is more than 5,000 years old, its relevance was, is and will remain forever. Our scriptures undoubtedly impart Vedic knowledge, but they also use simple examples to show how to imbue life with meaning. The Bhagavad Gita should not be used only for swearing oaths in the courtroom. It should be understood correctly, as it can help prevent the conflicts that lead us there. Allow me to say that it tells us how to live a meaningful life and teaches us how to die peacefully. It's a manual for living and dying. When we fall sick, we visit a doctor. He checks us and prescribes the necessary medications with certain dos and don'ts. In the same manner, whenever we are faced with questions about our spiritual life or our internal afflictions, we need the spiritual master's help to diagnose and prescribe the right path. However, the journey will have to be undertaken by only us. Just as the doctor cannot take medicines on our behalf or personally administer every dose, we need to assimilate the divine knowledge and act accordingly to attain Godhead.

Looking at our life as a whole, we can divide it into four parts: birth, childhood, youth and adulthood. The first stage is joyful, then comes success, followed by one's duties and finally self-discipline. As adults, we only seek happiness and are often childish in our approach. Age is no bar to learning. Shree Shuka Muni was just sixteen, whereas the sages seated in front of him, eager to hear his wisdom, were all more than a hundred years old. Spirituality is latent both in a child and an aged person.

The part on self-discipline has been divided into four parts:

1. Karma Yoga
2. Gyana Yoga

3. Dhyan or Hatha Yoga
4. Bhakti Yoga

All of them are intertwined. The Bhagavad Gita offers a well-defined, comprehensive outlook, presenting all the yogas distinctly yet in one another. Bhakti encompasses them all. A bhakta is both a karmi and a gyani. Bhakti teaches us to build and cement our relationship with God, who can be our son, brother or friend, father or teacher.

The devotee establishes a deeply personal bond with the Divine, to the extent that if you want to treat Him as your foe, He is willing to accept that. The world divides, but the Gita binds us with a string of divine love. Outwardly, the world is divided. Intrinsically, at the core, it is one and indivisible. It is like an atom. So many atoms fuse to form a molecule, but when we attempt to split the atom, an atomic fusion takes place and destroys everything. Similarly, today's strife-torn world needs the healing touch of divine love. The cracks need to be filled with the Fevicol or Araldite of divine love, our very lifeline and the core of our existence. All saints, acharyas, prophets and avatars talk about uniting the world. In the age of Kali, nearly 550 years ago, Shree Chaitanya Mahaprabhu termed kirtana as 'Sankirtana', that is, collective singing in one voice. The ideology permeating the material world today is one of oneself. However, the Vedas declare, '*Vasudhaiva kutumbhakam*'—the world is one family. The physical body, mind, intellect and the atman may appear as different entities, but the body is unified through Karma Yoga, the mind through Dhyana Yoga, the intellect through Gyana Yoga and the atman through Bhakti Yoga. So, in a way, the Gita is the text for unifying not only ourselves but also all of humanity.

Principally, this chapter can be divided into three parts. From verses 1 to 7, Shree Krishna describes His swaroopa. Verses 8 to 12 explain the different stages of bhakti, and verses 13 to 20 talk about the virtues of the bhakta, which He wants to see in His devotee.

Previously, the devotee was watching the Divine, and now, the Divine is watching over His devotee. Bhakti Yoga is the science of this union of the devotee and the Divine. The world entertains argument, whereas bhakti wants a dialogue or a discussion. Arguments give rise to disputes, and disputes separate people or even drive nations to war, as seen in the Mahabharata.

In the first shloka of this chapter, Arjuna, as our representative, asks Lord Krishna:

Evam satatyukta ye bhaktasttvam paryupaasattey|
Ye chaapyaksharamavyaktam tteysham kay yogavittamaha||
(Gita 12:1)

(Hey Bhagwan! Are the surrendered devotees those who are immersed in your Saguna Swaroopa and constantly absorbed in dhyana, who do your bhajan? Or are they those who are immersed in your Nirguna Swaroopa, considering you as the eternal, ever-blissful, formless Brahman. Out of the two, whom do you prefer?)

Arjuna specifically asks Lord Krishna, 'Yogavittamaha?' Who is truly united with the Divine, or who can be called the better devotee? Someone asked Swami Vivekananda whether he perceived the Supreme as masculine or feminine. He replied that it is a paradox: *'Jaaki rahi bhavana jaisi, Prabhu moorat dekhi tinha taisi* (One sees the paramatman according to his or her nature or perception).' Allow me to make a small submission here: in prema or divine love, the formless takes form, and the one with form becomes formless! It is like that age-old question: does the egg come first or the chicken? Those who walk the path of prema are unbothered about these things. Divine love has the power to see the beloved in the very form he or she loves. In other words, the beloved assumes the form his lover wants or vice versa. When Goswami Tulsidas Ji came to Vrindavan, he wanted to see Shree Gopal as Shree Rama, holding a bow and arrow in place of the flute. It is said that this incident took place at Gyana Guddadi (Vrindavan). In response to

Tulsidas Ji's formless being, omnipresent Divine assumed the form of Shree Rama, fulfilling his devotee's desire. Even today, those Goswamis who serve at the Shree Radha Raman temple often find themselves unable to complete the shringara (divine adornment). They need to go within, concentrate deeply and attune themselves to the image of the lord. Only then, when the service is performed, does Shree 'Lalju' accept it. Otherwise, it is impossible. This is no imagination.

It is my personal experience, and I request you all to try it for yourselves. Visualise the Divine form you love and intently focus on it. Gradually, your visualisation will transform into a true-to-life image before your eyes or in your heart. When we see the Shiva Lingam in the temple, it represents the form and the formless. In appearance, it has a shape. But that shape is the visualisation of nothingness or space. It is like a child moulding clay into various forms, only to mix it back into one undivided mass. The philosophical term for this is 'Achinttya Bhedabheda'.

Defining bhakti is no easy task. Still, it can be understood as devotion marked by a deep emotional connection to God. It comes from the Sanskrit root word 'bhaj', meaning 'to adore or worship God'. Bhakti Yoga is a real, heartfelt search for the lord which begins, continues and culminates in divine love. Rishi Shandilya defines bhakti as the attachment to the Lotus Feet of the Supreme. The Bhakti Rasamrita Sindhu thinks of bhakti as the means to engage all our senses and mind in the service of the Supreme Personality of Godhead, with the sole purpose of pleasing Him. Shree Krishna, being compassionately inclined towards us, in the second shloka says:

Maiyyaveshya mano ye maam nityayukta upaasattey|
Shraddhaya paryopeytasttey mey yuktattama mataha||
(Gita 12:2)

(Those who fix their mind on me, worship me, ever steadfast and endowed with supreme faith, they in my view are the best yogis.)

The saguna bhakta will say that his 'ishta' is omnipresent, while the nirguna bhakta will say that the Supreme permeates the entire creation. The formless, though infinite, is limited to being only without form. But for the one with form, the same Supreme manifested as Shree Radha Vallabh to Shree Harivansh, as Shree Bihari for Shree Haridas, as 'Shree Ji' for Shree Vallabh and Shree Radha Raman for Shree Roopa Sanatan-Jeeva Sripada Gopal Bhatt Goswami. They are the different swaroopas of Shree Krishna, but they all have different leela. The third and fourth shlokas talk about the characteristics of the Bramhavadis.

Ye tvaksharamanirdeshyam avaktam parupaasattey|
Sarvatragamchintyancha kootastham achallam dhruvam||
(Gita 12:3)

Sanniyamyendriyagramam sarvatra sama budhhayaha|
Ttey prapnuvanti maameva sarvabhoothittey rataaha||
(Gita 12:4)

(Those who worship me, the imperishable, the indefinable, the unmanifest, the omnipresent, the unthinkable, the unchangeable, the immovable and the eternal, having restrained all the senses, even-minded at all times, rejoicing in the welfare of all beings; verily come unto me.)

For example, the Govardhan Hill symbolises formlessness, whereas Shree Govardhan Nath possesses a form. Similarly, the Shaligram Shila denotes formlessness, but Shree Radha Raman Lal has a form. Shree Gopal Bhatt Goswami Maharaj's bhakti made it happen.

Firstly, the saguna bhakta does not need to exert control over his senses because he has the 'naam, leela, guna, dham and swaroopa' to enable him to focus his attention. On the other hand, the nirguna bhakta has no such mental support.

Secondly, the bhakta unconditionally surrenders himself at the Lotus Feet of the Lord. On the other hand, the gyani has to exercise control over his senses and focus his mind. Shree Ramanuj Acharya says that there are two types of bhaktis: one whose devotion is akin to a cat, and the other is that of a monkey. The cat holds the kitten by its teeth, but the baby monkey has to grasp their mother. The first is saguna bhakti, and the second is nirguna bhakti.

Thirdly, as we see in the case of Dhruva, he is a small child who doesn't know how to pray. But the lord imparts him divine knowledge, whereas in the case of a nirguni, he has to remove his ignorance.

Fourth, the lord liberates the saguna bhakta, while the nirguna bhakta has to strive for his liberation.

Fifth, the Chaitanya Charit Amrit says that merely uttering the divine name of the lord absolves us from our sins on the path of bhakti. However, if the gyani commits a mistake, he has to start all over again.

Sixth, the nirguna bhakta can experience the grace of the Divine instantly. The gyani cannot until he resonates with the reasoning of his consciousness.

Seventh, the saguni can unshackle himself from the bonds of karma by offering them to His Lordship. The nirguni must do all that is necessary to get out of the cycle of karma.

Eighth, for the saguna, divine love and trust are supreme. For the nirguna, total detachment is a must.

Ninth, the saguna bhakta offers everything to God and then uses it as prasad. The nirguna bhakta, when he becomes the enjoyer, becomes an impediment in the sadhana.

The eighth shloka is one of the most important ones in the Gita, and Lord Krishna extolls the highest form of devotion here.

Maiyyeva mann aadhatsva mayyi buddhim niveshaya|
Nivasishyasi mayyiyeva ata urdhvam na sanshayaha||
(Gita 12:8)

(Fix your mind on me alone, place your intellect in me, then you shall without any doubt abide in me alone.)

This is one of the highest stages of bhakti. Our texts and scriptures are filled with stories of bhakti. Such bhakti has been practised by the gopis of Braj, and since I am from Varanasi, I can relate to it very easily. Even herein, when Lord Krishna says, '*Sarva dharmaan paritajjya maamekkam sharannam vrajaha* (Relinquishing all ideas of righteousness, surrender unto Me alone)', the word 'vrajaha' for me is indicative of Braj, surrendering unto Shree Krishna, Braj Bhushan! All the bhaktas have attained this exalted state like Meera Bai, Shree Narsi Mehta, Tukaram and Namdev.

Atha chittam samadhattum na shaknoshi mayi sthiram|
Abhyasayogena tato matichhaptum Dhananjaya||
(Gita 12:9)

(If you are unable to fix your mind steadily on me, then by constant practice, seek to reach me, O Dhananjaya.)

If the mind cannot naturally fix itself on the Lord, then practise chanting His divine name, listening to His katha and kirtana, and participating in contemplation. Such practices will help us gradually focus our attention on the Lotus Feet of the Lord. From this verse to the tenth, Lord Krishna shares different paths to attain Him. For those who are more extroverted, He advises performing our duties sincerely as an offering unto Him, without any expectations. Taking it a step further, for those still driven by desires and seeking results, He instructs them to accept the result as a prasad and avoid any emotional reaction. In a way, the twelfth verse is the summarisation of verses 9 to 11. Here, Lord Krishna says: knowledge is indeed better than practice, meditation is better than knowledge, renunciation of the fruits of all actions is better than meditation, leading to everlasting peace. From verses 13 to 19, Shree Krishna clearly outlines the characteristics of one who has progressed through all the steps and discovered fulfilment. At this point, He is trying to simplify bhakti, making it accessible to even ordinary mortals like you and me. In these verses, He describes the traits of His Param Bhakta or the one who is most dear to Him. This has a dual purpose—firstly, as an inspiration for a true seeker to pursue his sadhana, and secondly, the natural traits of His dear devotee serve as practice guidelines for the rest. At the end of each verse, Lord Krishna affirms that such a bhakta is dear to Him.

We can broadly divide these verses into two sets, one set highlighting the virtues of the devotee, and the second set refers to those that should be shunned at any cost. They are as follows:

1. Verse 13: Maitri (friendliness) and Dvesha (hatred)
2. Verse 13: Karuna (compassion) and Maamakaara (mineness)
3. Verse 13: Samatvam (equanimity) and Ahankar (ego)
4. Verse 13: Kshama (forgiveness); Verse 15: Udvega (anxiety)
5. Verse 14: Santushti (contentment); Verse 15: Harsha (elation)
6. Verse 14: Yataatmatvam (self-control); Verse 15: Amarsha (envy)
7. Verse 14: Dridhanishchaya (firmness); Verse 15: Bhaya (fear)
8. Verse 14: Bhakti (devotion); Verse 16: Apeksha (expectation)
9. Verse 15: Mridu (gentleness); Verse 16: Anapeksha (indifferent)
10. Verse 16: Suchita (purity); Verse 17: Shoka (grief)
11. Verse 16: Dakshata (expertise); Verse 17: Aakanksha (desire)
12. Verse 16: Udaaseena (neutral); Verses 17, 18 and 29: Pairs of opposites (comfort and discomfort, honour and dishonour)

In essence, Lord Krishna enumerates the characteristics He wants to see in His bhakta, such as being merciful, free of malice, friendly, compassionate, unattached, un-egoistic, equipoised, forgiving, content, yogi, self-controlled, of firm conviction, who is not a source of hurt to anyone, unagitated, fearless, not expecting anything from anyone, pure, skilful, undisturbed, renouncing everything unto the lord and so on. Devarishi Narada declares in his bhakti aphorisms, *Yatha Braj gopikaanam* (Like the gopis of Braj), who are at an exalted position in the Prema Bhakti. These qualities came to them naturally. In the Vattrasura-Stuti, we see, '*Priyam priyeva vyshittam vishanna, manoarvindaksha didrikshattey ttvam* (A chaste wife whose husband is away from home and is never satisfied until and unless she sees her beloved)' (Shrimad Bhagavatam 6:11:26). In the present age, Prema Avatar Shree Chaitanya Mahaprabhu has shown the path of Prema Bhakti, which we all can follow.

This chapter, though short, has very deep and exhaustive connotations. Bhakti is as infinite as the lord Himself, and every school of thought or religion is filled with tales of devotion. Divine love is universal, and I would just like to add that bhakti, or love, unites. The world needs love in all spheres so that there can be unity. May the Divine grace fill our hearts with bhakti!

SUMMARY

Verses 1–7: Shree Krishna describes His swaroopa.
Verses 8–12: Description of different types of bhaktis.
Verses 13–20: The attributes Lord Krishna wants to see in His devotee.

KEY QUOTES

1. To express the actual emotion or feeling is very difficult.
2. Prema is beyond words; it cannot be explained.
3. The world divides, whereas the Gita unites.
4. Division creates arguments, whereas unity creates a dialogue.
5. The world sees progress in division, whereas spirituality, or bhakti, evolves in unity.
6. Prema can see a form in the formless or vice versa.
7. Where there is prema, knowledge follows.
8. The lord or the sadguru repeats again and again to make us understand.

13

Kshetra Kshetragya Vibhaga Yoga

The Yoga of the Field and Knower of the Field

Total verses: 35

The previous chapter offered a profound exploration of Bhakti Yoga, the path of devotion. Lord Krishna explains the supreme significance and the transformative power of devotion as the most accessible means to attain union with the Divine. Through bhakti, Lord Krishna emphasises how even an ordinary aspirant can rise to extraordinary spiritual heights.

Throughout the previous chapter, Shree Krishna describes the defining qualities of a bhakta: equanimity in pleasure and pain, contentment, self-restraint and unconditional love for all beings. Those who cultivate such virtues, surrender themselves unto Him and perform all actions with devotion and without attachment will certainly reach His supreme abode.

One of the most significant takeaways from that chapter is the inclusiveness of the path of devotion. Even those who approach the Divine with some material desires, if they remain sincere in their worship, will eventually progress on the path of bhakti. He promises that through such devotion, spiritual progress is inevitable, as the aspirant's heart becomes purified. As we move on to this chapter, Kshetra and Kshetragya Vibhaga Yoga (The Field and the Knower of the Field), the focus shifts from the path of emotional devotion to a more intellectual and philosophical inquiry into the nature of self and the material world.

I am a follower of the path of devotion, so it comes naturally to me. In my personal experience, gyana (knowledge) follows bhakti. We have analysed the doctrine of karma in the first six chapters, and bhakti in the last six. Now, we enter the realm of gyana. This demands a serious and thoughtful understanding to grasp its subtleties and intricacies. In my opinion, this chapter of the Bhagavad Gita has to be understood very minutely to comprehend the profound truths it contains. While the previous chapter emphasised the personal relationship between the devotee and the Divine, calling for a complete and unconditional surrender to His form, this chapter invites a deeper understanding. The transition highlights how Shree Krishna's teachings move fluidly from devotion to wisdom, guiding Arjuna and all the seekers towards a comprehensive vision of spiritual life. To sustain devotion and progress further, we also need wisdom. The word 'kshetra' means the field, and 'kshetragya' means the one who knows the field. Specifically, it is the knowledge of the nature of reality, and the interplay between the material and spiritual. It builds up to the devotional surrender in the eighteenth chapter by providing the intellectual tools necessary to understand who we are. This transition is essential—a devotee must not just feel love for God but also understand the underlying principles that govern this material world. The eternal soul is distinct from the body and the transient world. Lord Krishna leads Arjuna from a place of emotional surrender to the zone of intellectual clarity, ensuring that both His devotee's heart and mind are engaged in the pursuit of liberation.

Devotion without knowledge can be overly emotional, and knowledge without devotion can lead to dry intellectualism. Through His wisdom, Shree Krishna offers both approaches in a balanced way, enabling seekers to navigate the spiritual path holistically. In this chapter, Lord Krishna presents an in-depth analysis of the material body and the eternal soul. The body, mind and the senses belong to the kshetra, while the soul is kshetragya. The soul, being eternal, experiences the material world as being distinct from it. It remains indestructible and untouched by birth or death. Our material nature is known as 'prakriti', and the Supreme Consciousness is known as 'purusha'. Their interaction creates a world of experiences. Understanding this difference between matter and spirit is crucial for spiritual liberation, as it teaches us to detach from the fleeting material world and focus on the eternal soul.

Children enjoy playing with masks—the more distorted and grotesque the mask, the greater the thrill. The secret of this fun is the fact that they know that each mask is different, and they are immune to the aberrations of the other masks. In much the same way, we are an amalgam of matter and spirit. Body, mind and intellect are forms of matter. That which breathes life into the inert matter is the spirit. We are that spirit, the real face behind the mask. Interestingly, the word 'personality' comes from the Latin word 'persona', meaning mask. Ignorant of our true nature, we mistakenly identify the distortions and limitations of the material world with ourselves, and, as a result, suffer. Matter being inert is susceptible to outward influences. Nothing affects the spirit; it commands the world. Ignorance weakens us, making us slaves of the environment around us. Lord Krishna exhorts us to awaken and realise our glory.

The material world is temporarily given to us to play and enjoy, but instead it has become a source of distress, anguish and agony. Shree Krishna says, '*Vaasansi jeernanni yatha vihaaya* (As we discard old clothes).' He epitomises this state. Wearing the mask, He is endearing, charming, charismatic and adorned by all. The gopis, exasperated by His mischief, forget their anger when they see His captivating smile. Divested of the mask, He is awesome and worshipful as we have seen in the Vishwa-Roopa-Darshan.

All we need to understand is the difference between the mask and our true self. Once we do, the distortions of the material world become entertaining, and our interface with the world becomes perfect. We become a repository of grace, happiness and power. For example, if I know how to paint, then I can paint any picture I want. But if I don't know how to paint, even drawing a straight line will be difficult. This chapter of the Gita makes us a 'somebody' from being a 'nobody'.

This chapter begins with Arjuna asking Shree Krishna the difference between matter and spirit, the field and knower of the field, and that which is to be known.

Prakritim purusham chaiva khsetram kshetragyameva cha|
Aetadveditumichhami Gyanam gyaeyam Keshava||
(Gita 13:1)

(Arjuna asks, 'O Keshava! I wish to know what is the difference between the matter and spirit, the field and the knower of the field, knowledge and that which ought to be known.')

This entire chapter explains these six queries. Shree Chakravarty Pada says that in the field of karma, grow the crop of dharma. This is the Gita's essence. Shree Krishna's brilliant exposition delineates the two so systematically that this chapter stands out in its clarity. Giving the analogy of the field, He says, 'The body is the kshetra or the field. Know me as the kshetragya, the knower in all the fields.'

He then divides the field or the matter into thirty-one segments. The spirit is different from them.

Kshetragyam chaapi maam viddhi sarvakshetreshu Bharata|
Khestrakshetragya yorgyaanam yattajgyaanam mattam muma||
(Gita 13:3)

(Know me as the knower of the field in all the fields, O Bharata; knowledge of the field as also of the knower of the field is considered by me to be my knowledge.)

Shree Krishna now talks about the Brahma Sutra, providing subtle explanations. During the dialogue between Rai Ramananda and Shree Chaitanya Mahaprabhu, He encourages them to ask anything they like within the realm of scriptures. We all need a guide in our lives. Many negate its requirement and dismiss the guidance. But in reality, it doesn't work that way. Our guru and the scriptures are like a mirror which shows us our face as it is. From verses 8 to 12, Lord Krishna enumerates twenty attributes which He would like to see in a gyani:

1. Humility
2. Unpretentiousness
3. Non-violence
4. Tolerance
5. Simplicity
6. Guru sewa
7. Purity
8. Steadfastness
9. Self-control
10. Indifference towards sensory pleasures
11. Renunciation
12. Devoid of ego
13. Understanding birth, death, old age, illness and pain
14. Non-attachment

15. Detached from wealth and familial connections
16. Equipoised
17. Unswerving devotion towards God
18. Reveling in solitude
19. Constantly striving to attain self-knowledge
20. Seeker of Truth

Lord Krishna declares that all this is knowledge, and all else is ignorance. Brahman alone is all that needs to be known—gyeyam, the supreme knowledge or the ultimate goal. Shree Krishna gives a brilliant description of Brahman using paradoxical terms, as He is beyond the grasp of the intellect. Shree Chaitanya Mahaprabhu aptly captures this in one shloka: *'Trinnadapi suneechena tarrorapi sahishnuna, amaanina maan dena keertaneeya sada Hari* (One should chant the holy name of the lord with humility, thinking of oneself to be even lower than a tiny blade of grass, even more tolerant than a tree, devoid of all self-pride and should respect all).' I remember how once many great acharyas approached my sadguru maharaj and said that he was the foremost acharya of the Gaudiya sect, and that they wanted to anoint him as jagadguru. With utmost humility, he replied that there was only one jagadguru, Shree Krishna—'Bless me that I attain His Prema, that's enough for me! This is humility!'

If one possesses all the above, that would be perfect. But even if one of these qualities is present in us, we enter the realm of knowledge. From verses 13 to 18, Shree Krishna explains what needs to be known or knowable. In the sixteenth verse, He says;

Bahirantashcha bhootanam acharam charameva cha|
Sookshmatvattad vigyeyam duurastham chaantikay cha tatt||
(Gita 13:16)

(Without and within all beings, the unmoving and also the moving; because of the subtlety of the unknowable, near yet far away, it is That.)

Here, I am referring to Sankhya Yoga. The Supreme dwells within all beings, yet He appears to be very far. Shree Prahalad tells Hiranyakashipu that there is nothing devoid of His presence. He is within you and without. When there is a crack in the wall, it may fall. On the other hand, a crack in our hearts builds more walls! When there is prema, even the one who is far away seems very, very close. Devoid of prema, the closest one seems distant. Shree Krishna distinguishes between prakriti (matter) and purusha (spirit). While the spirit remains the same, matter changes. The spirit expresses itself differently in different people. In the evil, it is a mere witness. As one cleanses oneself, the spirit becomes the approver and protector, fulfilling one's endeavours as he becomes unselfish. Further, it enables us to enjoy the world and wield power. In the end, when one removes all obstacles, the spirit will reveal itself as the Supreme Self. The lord assures us all that one who understands the nature of purusha and prakriti is not born again, whatever his lifestyle. He becomes a spirit. We attain liberation by eliminating desires through action. Subtle desires are sublimated through knowledge, and their last traces are removed by meditation. The ignorant, incapable of coming onto this path, can still evolve and go beyond death by surrendering to the guru. And the one who sees the Supreme Spirit acting in everything attains self-realisation.

The spirit neither acts. Nor is it tainted by actions. It remains untouched like space and illumines the entire creation like the sun. Therefore, develop the gyana chakshu, the eye of wisdom, and we shall perceive the difference between the spirit and matter, merging with the Supreme.

Kshetra khsetragya yorevam antaram gyana chakshusha|
Bhoot prakriti moksham cha ye viduryanti ttey param||
(Gita 13:35)

(Those with their eyes of wisdom come to know the distinction between the field and the knower of the field, attain liberation from this prakriti merging in the Supreme.)

As I often repeat this famous Gaudiya line, '*Jeever swaroopa hoya nitya Krishna das* (The true nature of jeeva is being in the constant service of Shree Krishna).' The Brahma Samhita says, '*Ishwara param Krishnaha sarvakaaranakaarannam* (Shree Krishna is the Supreme, the prime cause of this entire creation).' The dedicated study of these spiritual texts cleanses our mind, inclining it towards the lord. A bhakta may seem strange, but his life is very simple and humble, and he sees Shree Krishna all around him, everywhere, in everything. This body is the field. The soul is the knower of the field. Shree Krishna is the Supreme Personality of Godhead. The principal object of knowledge is the lord, and the subject matter of this knowledge is the study of these twenty-five elements: five organs of action, five organs of sensory knowledge, five subtle elements (shabd, roopa, rasa, gandha and sparsh), the mind, intellect, chitta and ahankara, adding up to twenty-four, and the twenty-fifth being the jeeva. There is also the twenty-sixth, which is the Paramatman Tattva. Therefore, the principal driving force of these twenty-five is the Almighty, who is to be known and realised.

As we move from bhakti to intellectual enquiry, we are reminded that the spiritual path requires both love and discernment. Shree Krishna's divine words lead us towards the ultimate realisation of our true nature and our eternal relationship with the Divine. This chapter very subtly guides us on the path of sadhana. We must strive for the truth. With hard work and His divine grace, we can climb the ladder of Godhood. By practice, we will learn that this body is not our real self. Unless we start perceiving the Divine and the one abiding in everyone, there will be no unity.

SUMMARY

Verses 1–7:	The difference between the field and the knower of the field.
Verses 8–12:	The explanation of gyana.

Verses 13–19: The explanation of the subject matter of gyana.
Verses 20–26: The explanation of 'prakriti' and 'purusha'.
Verses 27–35: The explanation of 'gyana chakshu'.

KEY QUOTES

1. Prema attains fulfilment when both the lover and the beloved complement each other.
2. The point of conflict is desire and envy.
3. Grow the crop of dharma in the field of karma.
4. Whatever your point of contention, it should find a reference in the scriptures.
5. The guidance of the guru and scriptures is essential in life.
6. When there is a crack in the wall, it falls, and when there is a crack in the heart, it builds walls.
7. Entirely surrendered bhakti is only possible through divine grace.
8. You can't progress if you go on comparing yourself with others.
9. The Gita tells us the difference between spirit and matter.

14

Guna Traya Vibhaga Yoga
The Three Qualities of Material Nature
Total verses: 27

We are all on this divine journey of the Shrimad Bhagavad Gita, trying to understand the deeper meanings hidden in the words of this profound text. Honestly, we cannot acquire divine knowledge only by reading, studying or reciting. It can only be attained through the divine grace of our sadguru, and I am an example of the same. I am no scholar or philosopher, that I can speak on a complex text like the Gita. Whatever I am sharing is only through the benevolent grace of sadguru. I am merely an instrument, and He is revealing whatever you and me can comprehend. In reality, *'Krishnam vanddey Jagadgurum'* (Shree Krishna alone is the Supreme Master).

In the thirteenth chapter, we learnt how ignorance of our true self creates the illusory but distinct entity, jeeva. The jeeva is entrapped as a result of its attachment to prakriti, which is an amalgam of three gunas (sattva, rajas and tamas). The way out of this quagmire of the gunas is shown herein. We have two words: jai (material victory) and vijay (mastering the senses). By Shree Krishna's grace, Arjuna first attained vijay and then won the Mahabharata war.

We are now studying the intricacies of gyana. Lord Krishna glorifies the knowledge that leads us to moksha or liberation. It has already been clarified that the amalgamation of the awareness aspect and the material aspect of Ishvara is the primary cause of this creation. The purusha, present within us as the jeeva, identifies itself with prakriti, that is, the material world. The confusion, born of ignorance, binds the jeeva in an endless cycle of birth and death. We are all blessed with divinity, but it is never stable or constant; it is always in a state of flux, increasing or decreasing. I can serve the Divine by worshipping in a temple, and also by offering my words as a service to the Divine from my heart. This realisation is the prasad of bhakti, universal love, and has been explained in the previous chapter. There is a difference between what we do and what we are capable of doing. The Bhagavad Gita helps us achieve excellence in the world, and it takes us to a state of enlightenment. It is a thorough analysis of the human personality, identifying the areas of weakness and eradicating them. We are all made of matter and spirit.

The Gita sieves the matter, and what remains is pure spirit. The spirit is all-pervading. A mere nudge ignites the divinity within, and a little girl goes on to become Meera Bai, or a young Prince Siddhartha becomes Gautama Buddha. Human potential is immense, and Shree Krishna simply awakens Arjuna to realise his own. Matter comprises three distinct characteristics or gunas. They are sattva (purity), rajas (passion) and tamas (ignorance). They determine the quality of our thoughts, emotions and actions. Together, they bind us to the material world. Like the three primary colours—red, yellow and blue—when mixed give us newer hues, the combination of these gunas creates the infinite variety of beings in the world. An animal cannot transcend the realm of the three gunas, but we humans do. To undermine or to spoil is very easy, but to create or to rise above the ordinary calls for effort. That is why it is called extraordinary.

Tamas is a state of inertia and indifference. In this condition, even the finest qualities are shrouded, and our inherent talent is stifled from manifesting. Rajas is a state of stress and agitation brought by greed, craving and lust. The incessant, desire-fuelled activity and resulting mental turbulence give rise to mediocrity. Sattva is the tranquillity of the mind when one functions at their best. This is a state that all executives, sportspersons and professionals in every field strive for—being in the 'zone', performing at the peak of excellence. Yet few know how to achieve it, and fewer still know how to sustain it. The Bhagavad Gita spells it out clearly and simply so that everyone can operate from sattva while marginalising and eventually eliminating rajas and tamas. Tamasic is a state of deep sleep, rajasic is dozing off, whereas sattvic is fully awake. This chapter explains how the gunas bind us. In Sanskrit, guna means rope. We all have these three within us. As long as we remain oblivious to their nature and influence, we are bound by them. When we understand them, we can alter their percentage within us. We excel when sattva predominates. Rajas breeds greed, disquiet and hankering for more, and when tamas reigns supreme, we are in a state of delusion, heedlessness and inertia.

The scriptures say that the devas are sattvic, man is rajasic and the demons are tamasic. God has blessed us with the capacity to decrease or increase the influence of each of these within us, and that is the message of this chapter. Lord Shiva's trident represents the three gunas, which form the prakriti. He is Isha, the master of this creation. We have the trimurti, Brahma, Vishnu and Shiva, and there are many references to the trio in our scriptural texts. Shree Krishna explains that the gunas' relative strength also determines the realm we enter after death. A sattvic person is born as a bhakta in a spiritual family where the sattva quality blossoms in an ambience of purity and tranquillity. However, it may take many births to completely eradicate the traces of rajas and tamas. Pure sattva catapults us into the state of self-realisation. The rajasic is born amongst people attached to action and gets further entrenched in the materialistic world. The tamasic is born a dull fool. Each soul progresses according to the predominance of their guna. The sattvic progresses on the spiritual path like the eight-lane expressway, the rajasic on a single-lane road, while the tamasic goes downhill. Our life's objective is to go beyond the three gunas and attain liberation from the cycle of birth, death, decay and sorrow. We are intrinsically immortal and need to realise it in this very birth.

Param bhooya pravakshyami gyaananaam gyanmuttamam|
Yajgyatva munayaha sarvey paraam siddhimitto gataha||
(Gita 14:1)

Iddam gyanmupashritya muma saadharmya maagataha|
Sarggeyapi nopajaayanttey pralaye na vyathanti cha ||
(Gita 14:2)

(Shree Krishna says, 'I am again declaring that supreme knowledge, which has been known by all the sages who have attained the supreme goal. Those who have taken refuge in this knowledge have attained me; they are neither reborn at the time of creation nor do they get disturbed at the time of dissolution.')

Lord Krishna stresses surrendering unto His supreme knowledge. But in the eighteenth chapter, He says, '*Sarva dharman parityajjya maamekam sharannam vraja* (Leaving everything else, just seek my refuge).' Supreme knowledge will lead us to the Supreme. Goswami Tulsidas Ji says in the Ramcharitmanas, *'Jaaney binu na hoi pariteeti| Binu pariteeti hoi nahi preeti* (Without knowing one cannot have conviction and without conviction, one cannot love).' Shree Krishna asks us to continue on the path of knowledge and strive to attain the Supreme. As we move on this path with dedication and faith, a stage comes when the Supreme is revealed. He further adds:

> *Sarvayonishu Kauntteya moortayaha sambhavanti yaha|*
> *Taasam Brahma mahadyoniraham beejapradaha pita||*
> (Gita 14:4)

(It should be understood that all the species, O son of Kunti, that are born in this material world, I am the seed-implanting father of this creation.)

Lord Krishna declares that prakirti is the mother, and He is the father. As a person receives genes from both parents, the physical body, mind and the intellect are from the prakriti, and the 'Atman Tattva' is from the purusha. When two bodies unite, the 'jeeva-atma' is born. When two souls unite, a mahatma is born. When two mahatmas unite, then Shree Rama or Shree Krishna takes birth.

> *Sattvam rajastama iti gunaha prakriti sambhavaha|*
> *Nibadghnanti Mahabaaho dehey dehinamavyayam||*
> (Gita 14:5)

(Purity, passion and inertia are the three gunas of the prakriti, which bind the atman in the body.)

From time to time, each guna will try to suppress the others and gain prominence. This chapter is about self-discipline and self-discovery. A key concept here is attention regulation, our ability to manage where or how we can focus our mind. At one extreme is a distraction, where the mind is scattered in different directions. The other extreme is obsession when the attention is fixated on one thing to the point of becoming oblivious to everything else. It's as dangerous and unwise as driving while looking at your phone! The ideal is intentional focus or active attention on a specific task or goal with a purpose. Watching TV and reading a book are two different things. While watching, the external imaginary world is created before us, but while reading a book, we have to create this world of imagination, which requires additional effort. That is why TV is also referred to as the idiot box! Modes shape our external and internal experiences. The modes are thus associated with both external stimuli and the internal state of mind. Over time, we become habituated to functioning in ways shaped by the dominant mode. However, modes can change naturally or intentionally. For example, mornings are mostly sattvic, afternoons are rajasic and nights are tamasic. These can be intentionally altered by our habits.

Today, we seem to know the world, but we don't know ourselves, thereby neglecting the most important part of our journey. A homogeneous mixture of the three helps us lead a meaningful life. However, Lord Krishna emphasises the sattva guna over the other two, for it will lead us towards the supreme goal. We need to leverage tamas and rajas as stepping stones to the realm of sattva: '*Ati sarvatra varjayeta* (An excess of everything is bad)'. When asked what is poison, Swami Vivekananda had answered, 'Excess of anything or everything is poison!'

From verses 5 to 9, Shree Krishna analyses the three gunas, and from verses 11 to 18, He presents a synthesis of all three, explaining their drawbacks and short-term and long-term benefits. Our conduct is within the realm of these three, and the atman is a mere spectator.

Verses 19 and 20 explain this phenomenon and state that one who can transgress these three will not be stuck in the rut of birth, old age and death. He will attain supreme bliss.

In the twenty-first shloka, Arjuna asks three questions: what are the qualities of the one who is beyond the realm of the three gunas? How does this person behave? And, how can I transgress these three? From verses 22 to 26, Shree Krishna answers these questions. Firstly, the individual is disinterested or passive in whatever is happening around them. In other words, the person is neutral. Then there is equanimity, or being balanced in all situations—whether it is favourable or unfavourable. Being balanced is the nature of the 'trigunateeta'.

> *Maam cha yoavyabhichaarena bhaktiyogena sevatey|*
> *Sa gunnansamatittyatan Brahmbhooyayah kalpatey||*
> (Gita 14:26)

(And he serving me with unswerving devotion and crossing over the three gunas is fit to attain Brahman.)

> *Brahmanno he prattishthaham mritasyavyayasya cha|*
> *Shaasvattasya cha dharmasya sukhasyyaikaantikasya cha||*
> (Gita 14:27)

(For I am the abode of Brahman, the immortal and the immutable, everlasting dharma and absolute bliss.)

The final part of this chapter describes a person who has transcended the gunas. It leads us to the Bramhapada. When we experience this interplay of the gunas and remain unaffected, we go beyond the realm of maya and attain enlightenment. Lord Krishna imparts the knowledge that will enable us to overcome His 'trigunamayi maya', and this is only possible if we unconditionally surrender unto Him. With a focused mind, without any selfish motives, surrendering at the Lotus Feet of Shree Krishna leads us to His divine abode.

However, Shree Krishna's message is that through conscious effort and spiritual practice, we have the power to guide our consciousness from ignorance to pure knowledge, from tamas to sattva, ultimately transcending all three into spiritual realisation. The initial configuration of sattva, rajas and tamas in one's psyche is not accidental. It is a continuum of experience and energy carried forward from one life to the next. In conjunction with the Gita, the Vedic texts, such as the Upanishads and the commentaries of the acharyas, elaborate on how these modes are not arbitrary but are carefully determined by past karmas. Their percentages within us are not fixed, and they are constantly vying for supremacy. Because of their fluctuating state, it is not certain that a person who is currently more sattvic will remain so indefinitely. The influence of the environment, food, our associations and daily activities shapes which guna will be prominent at any given time. That is why Lord Krishna stresses Abhyasa Yoga, or consistency in our spiritual practices. In fact, our goal is to transcend all three. Shree Krishna emphasises the urgency of spiritual striving. Rather than squandering this birth on mere sense gratification, we must invest in spiritual practices like japa, dhyana or bhakti. Such efforts, sustained over time, restructure the mind towards transcendence.

Our thoughts possess momentum. According to the law of attraction as taught by Abraham Hicks, when we think of something for seventeen seconds, it gains enough momentum to continue thinking. So, if we hold onto positive thoughts for a sustained period, they gather strength and eventually become habitual. Eventually, this subtle shift in mental hygiene can move our inner equilibrium towards goodness. An integrated understanding will inspire us to apply these principles in our daily life, transforming it into an opportunity for spiritual growth and realising Brahman beyond the realm of all the gunas. Lord Krishna is guiding our soul from darkness to light, from restlessness to peace, and from limitation to infinite freedom.

SUMMARY

Verses 1–2:	The glory of gyana.
Verses 3–4:	The explanation of how the atman enters this world.
Verses 5–8:	The introduction of the three gunas.
Verses 9–10:	The conclusion of the different phases.
Verses 11–13:	The definition of the three gunas.

Verses 14–18:	The analysis, combination and synthesis.
Verses 19–20:	The effect of the gunas.
Verses 21–26:	The answer to Arjuna's three questions.
Verse 27:	Bhakti is beyond the realm of the gunas and is supreme.

KEY QUOTES

1. How will one follow the words if one cannot comprehend the silences?
2. Without the guru's grace, one cannot attain gyana.
3. We can either serve through words or worship.
4. The Gita is the sutra for enriching the humaneness of humans.
5. Outward victory is jai; inner victory is vijay.
6. The Gita extols us to do what we can do best!
7. The Atman Tattva unites, whereas the material world separates.
8. To do evil is easy, but to do noble deeds is tough.
9. If someone else can do it, then why can't we?
10. We don't realise that we have infinite possibilities.

15

Purushottam Yoga

The Yoga of the Divine

Total verses: 20

The fifteenth chapter of the Bhagavad Gita is unique in several ways. Both the chapter on Bhakti Yoga and this chapter, Purushottam Yoga, consist of only twenty verses. In my opinion, they are both the most significant portions of this great text. The seed is tiny, but it carries within it a giant banyan tree. In the same way, Shree Krishna narrates the essence of bhakti and Himself, the Purushottama, very precisely. Each letter and even the space between each word has a profound truth that can only be comprehended by His Divine grace. This chapter summarises the essence of the Gita and the Vedas. The cycle of birth, death, old age and illness goes on. First, the seed sprouts, then a tree is formed, the leaves and fruits fall, the tree decays and a new tree appears in its place. This is the pattern of the material world, but in spirituality or bhakti, or scriptural studies, the deeper we go, the more we grow. A lamp held closer will illuminate our surroundings. The Gita being a divine lamp, the closer it is to our lives, we more we are enlightened by its presence. It is a manual covering all the different facets of existence.

Specifically, this chapter covers four topics: what is the world, who am I, what is God (that is, what transcends the world and me) and what is the relationship between me, the world and God? These are the essentials of any scriptural study. Till the thirteenth chapter, we understand that the world of matter is one homogeneous entity, and the spirit is non-dual and infinite. The variations in the expression of the same spirit and matter in different individuals are on account of the interplay of the three gunas. The previous chapter concluded by stating that worshipping the lord with unwavering love leads to liberation. However, this is not possible without complete detachment.

To lead us to this state, Shree Krishna now discusses the nature of the spirit in all its manifestations. He explains the unknown from the known objects of perception, emotion and thought. He elaborates on the nature of Brahman and how it pervades this manifested world. Brahman is self-effulgent. It is visualised as the trinity of the perishable, imperishable and the uttama purusha or the Supreme. The infinite is defined as the imperishable 'akshara', concerning the perishable 'kshara' form of matter. With the imagery taken from the Kathopanishad, Lord Krishna portrays the entire universe as the ashwath, or the inverted peepul tree, with its roots above and branches below. The root represents the Brahman, the wielding power of prakriti, the Saguna Brahman, the eternal essence with attributes, and the branches are the universe. The growth of the secondary root that emerges from the main root is vasana, or ignorance. The branches are the different modes of the material world that either rise, taking us towards evolution, or grow downwards towards degradation. Shree Krishna tells Arjuna to cut off the firmly rooted tree of the material world with the axe of detachment or dispassion. To cultivate this detachment, we must go straight to the roots and seek refuge in the Parameshwara. We will need to shed our ego and delusions. Speaking of the kshetra, the kshetragya and Brahman, He explains the superiority of the Supreme Personality of Godhead—why He is the Supreme, the value of knowing Him and how He can be realised. Hence, this chapter is called the Purushottam Yoga. Exploring Purushottam from the perspective of bhakti, Shree Radha Raman or Shree Jagannath are regarded as Purushottam, and the Jagannath Puri is also known as the Purushottam Kshetra. My simple understanding is this: to become a uttama purusha, or attain perfection in life, is the primary objective of the Bhagavad Gita. To lead a meaningful life, we must correctly ascertain the purpose of our human birth. All of us are accustomed to travelling with some baggage. These days, we often face restrictions on the weight and size of the luggage. So, it is always advised to travel light. This is especially true for mountaineers; as they ascend towards the summit, they carry the least amount of baggage, knowing that a heavy load would make the climb difficult. In the same way, Lord Krishna urges us to reduce our burden as much as possible, leading to total dispassion. When Socrates was asked what dies, the soul or the body, he apologetically answered that he hadn't experienced death. Only if he died could he answer the question. He had detached himself so completely that even death was a celebration for him. In our tradition, a person who has given up the material world while maintaining control over the senses is called a swami. There are four basic principles in life:

1. The right judgement or wisdom controls the mind and the senses.
2. Strive to give, not to take.
3. Work towards unity, not division.
4. Think of what is permanent and what is not.

While studying the Gita, I sense a kaleidoscopic description. Visualise it yourself, and you will understand what I am trying to say. We will have to study this chapter as the continuation of the previous chapter. In the twenty-sixth verse of the last chapter, Lord Krishna says, '*Maam cha yoavyabhicharena bhaktiyogena sevattey* (Only the bhakta can transcend the realm of the three gunas and declare His preference in accepting bhakti as supreme).' He prefers devotion and detachment from the world. He indulges His devotee and helps him transcend the material world. Bhajan instils devotion and eradicates all that is worthless: '*Aaddau shraddha tatoartha bhajan kriya anarthanivritti* (In the beginning, one must have faith, which leads to interest in satsang. This helps one become free from unwanted habits and become firmly fixed in devotional practice)' (*Chaitanya Charitamitra*, Madhya Leela 23: 14–15). In the Shrimad Bhagavatam, Shree Shukadeva Ji Maharaj says, '*Uttamshloka leelaya*'—referring to the description of the pastimes of the Uttam shloka, the one who is the recipient of the highest form of worship: Shree Krishna. Similarly, the uttam purusha is the lord. In bhajan, the moment we utter the divine name, then naam, guna, leela and dham naturally enter the realm of our thoughts. The intellect starts to accept the divine reality, and all the ills dissipate. The divine name has an all-around effect. The Supreme and His name are the same. Shree Krishna says:

Urdhvamoolamadhaha shaakham Aswattham praahuravyayam|
Chhandasi yasya parnnani yasttam Veda sa vedavitt||
(Gita 15:1)

(The wise speak of the indestructible ashwath or the peepul tree, with the roots above and the branches below, the leaves are the meters or the hymns. The one who knows this is the knower of the Vedas.)

In Vibhuti Yoga, Lord Krishna has already declared, 'Amongst the trees, I am the ashwath.' In a way, He is elaborating on His vibhuti. When we see the reflection of the tree in a lake, the image is inverted. Here, the metaphor of an inverted tree is used to depict the transience of the material plane. It advocates detachment and spiritual wisdom. The lord begins with the perishable, that is, the external universe and the individual, while Brahman is the innermost essence of both. He reinforces the truth that we are the spirit acting through matter. When the spirit identifies with prakriti, the individual is born. It becomes attracted to the external universe, and the mind is clothed with the physical body. Upon leaving the body, it carries dormant desires as well as the subtle body, mind and the intellect. The ignorant fail to perceive the truth and are tossed about by the material changes in the world. Only the wise who see the underlying reality experience everlasting peace. From verses 1 to 3, Lord Krishna describes this ashwath tree, saying:

> *Na roopamasyeha tathhopalabhatey,*
> *Naanto na chaadirna cha samprattishtha|*
> *Aswathmeynnam suviroodhamoolam,*
> *Asangashastrena dridhena chhitwa||*
> (Gita 15:3)

(Its form is not perceived here as such; neither its end nor the origin, nor its foundation, nor the resting place. Cut this firm-rooted tree with the axe of non-attachment.)

Ashwath also means temporary. The phenomenal world is compared to the peepul because of its ever-changing nature. Typically, a tree's roots grow downwards into the earth. Here, it is just the opposite. The branches of this inverted tree represent the cosmic mind, ego, the five elements and the other cosmic principles which extend downwards. Just as the leaves protect the tree, the Vedas serve to protect and sustain the tree of the world. Creation exists on both sides of this tree: above lies the spiritual realm, while the world below is just the reflection.

Jagadguru Shankaracharya declared, '*Brahma satyam jagat mithya* (Brahman is the truth and the world is illusory).' Shree

Krishna explains that this tree, which represents creation, is endless—no one can comprehend its origin or its end. The sole purpose of human birth is to reach the supreme goal. This can only be possible when one surrenders to Him, and it is only through divine grace that one attains Him. Now, Shree Krishna is narrating the methodology:

Nirmanmoha jitsangadosha,
Adhyatmanitya vinivrittikamaha|
Dwandairvimuktaha sukhadukha sanggyair,
Gachhantya moodhaha padamavyayam tatt||
(Gita 15:5)

(Free from pride and delusion, victorious over the evil of attachment, dwelling constantly in the self, exercising strict control over all desires, free from all the dualities such as pleasure and pain, the undeluded reach their ultimate goal.)

Na tadbhaasayattey Suryo na shashanko na paavakaha|
Yadgatva na nivarnattey taddhama paramam muma||
(Gita 15:6)

(Nor does the sun shine there, neither the moon nor the fire; this is my supreme abode from where there is no return.)

Unless we accept both praise and criticism equally, we cannot move forward. The Chaitanya Charit Amrit states, '*Pratishtha sookari vishtha* (Name and fame is like pig waste).' Srila Prabodha Chandra Saraswati says, '*Sanmanam kalayeti ghor garalam neechapamaanam sudha* (When you hear your praises, think it to be poison, and when you are riled, consider it to be amrit).' The one who remains equipoised, both in praise and criticism, is like Lord Shiva. Although love and attachment are very close, they are two different things. In moha, one thinks about self. In prema, he thinks about the beloved. Bhajan needs practice until it becomes our nature. When it becomes effortless, only then is it a bhajan. We need to rise above dualities such as happiness and sorrow, pleasure and pain, cold and hot and so on. Lord Buddha insisted that all the bhikkhus go out every morning and seek alms. The primary purpose behind this was to annihilate the ego lying dormant within. Sewa is a great equaliser and helps to control anger, moha or pride. From verses 6 to 11, Lord Krishna explains the journey of the soul.

Mammaivansho jeevlokey jeevbhootaha sanatanaha|
Manaha shasthanindriyaani prakritisthani karshati||
(Gita 15:7)

(An eternal part of me, having become the living entity and abiding in jeeva–prakriti, draws to itself the five senses and the mind.)

From an absolute standpoint, the state of the individual soul is that there is one eternal essence, one consciousness or one self. However, just as a space appears to be divided into many walls, this eternal essence seems fragmented through apparent limitations or upadhis. By identifying with these limitations, an illusory identity emerges, imagining itself to be the jeeva. It takes on new forms to exhaust its endless desires, but unfortunately, this cycle is endless. Only the wise ones, those who have assimilated the teachings of the scriptures after purifying their minds through karma and Bhakti Yoga, realise the true nature of the self. All others live in delusion. Till the tenth verse, Shree Krishna elaborates on the different stages of the jeeva, who becomes entangled due to the effect of maya. In the eleventh verse, He directs the way out of this entanglement.

Yattanto yoginashchainam pashyanttatmanyavasthitam|
Yattantoapyakritatmano nainam pashyantachetasaha||
(Gita 15:11)

(The seekers striving for perfection behold me dwelling in the self; but, the unrefined and unintelligent, even though striving, don't see me.)

The one who is free from illusion and false prestige and association understands the Eternal Supreme. Who is done with material lust and is free from the duality of happiness and sorrow surrenders to the Supreme Personality of Godhead, thereby attaining Him. The splendour of the sun or the moon or the fire that illumines the entire world emanates from Him. He permeates the creation and sustains it.

Sarvasya chaaham hridi sannivishto,
Mattaha smritirgyan mapohanashcha|
Vedaishcha sarvayrahameva veddyo,
Vedantkrid vedavideva chaaham||
(Gita 15:15)

(I am seated in the hearts of all, and from me are the memory, knowledge as well as their absence. I am that which is known in all the Vedas. I am the author of Vedanta, and I am the Veda.)

Lord Krishna blesses us with smriti, or awareness. He clarifies that I give you the awareness, followed by wisdom and self-realisation: 'Smriti gyana apohanam.' Trishna and Krishna are both in front of us. When we face desire, Shree Krishna is behind us and vice versa. Verses 16–18 form the Trishloki Gita. The lord explains the gist of Vedanta in these three verses.

Dwavimau purushau lokay ksharshchakshara eva cha|
Ksharaha sarvaani bhootani kootastho akshara uchyatey||
(Gita 15:16)

(There are two types of jeevas, the perishable and the imperishable. All are perishable, but the Supreme Soul is imperishable.)

To dispel any false notion of the Brahman being perishable, Shree Krishna goes on to describe it as akshara. Brahman is the imperishable foundation of the perishable world. He sustains all beings with energy, nourishes them and is the fire that digests all that is consumed. Memory, knowledge and even their loss arise from Him. The sorrow and the pain of separation are mitigated by forgetfulness. This loss of memory is partial during life and complete at death. It is a great blessing, as it lightens the burden of life, otherwise it would be impossible to shoulder. It allows us to begin afresh on the journey of life and discover the hidden truths. Thus, He sustains both the macrocosm, the universe and the microcosm. Lord Krishna says that Brahman is akshara, the imperishable supporter of this perishable word. The sixteenth verse talks about the Jeeva Tattva, the seventeenth talks of the Paramatman Tattva and the seventeenth explains the Purushottama. In the material world, everything is perishable, and in the spiritual world, everything is imperishable. The param purusha is Shree Krishna, Purushottama. The one who knows this renders devotional service to Him in all respects. This profound teaching has been taught by the lord. Knowing this, one is illumined and accomplishes all that is needed.

Iti guyatammam shastram iddamuktam mayanagha|
Taddbuddhva buddhimanasyat kratkratyashcha Bharata||
(Gita 15:20)

(This secret teaching has been taught by me, and on knowing this, one becomes wise and accomplishes all the duties, O Bharata.)

In conclusion, the sole objective of this chapter, as I understand it, is that we need to withdraw our senses from the material world and focus our minds on the Divine. It may come across as futile, but we should at least strive to move towards the lord. Some practical tips we learn from this chapter include practising detachment, cultivating discernment, embracing humility and simplicity, seeking higher knowledge, living righteously, meditating regularly, serving others and surrendering unto Shree Krishna. By consistently applying them, we can navigate life with greater clarity and purpose, ultimately leading to liberation.

SUMMARY

Verses 1–5:	The description of the ashwath tree.
Verse 6:	God-realisation through total detachment.
Verses 7–11:	Transmigration ultimately leads to liberation.
Verses 12–15:	Divine guidance.
Verses 16–18:	Trishloki Gita.
Verses 19–20:	One who knows this, ultimately knows Him.

KEY QUOTES

1. The Bhagavad Gita talks about creating a balance in life.
2. The thought of giving and doing charity makes you a king.
3. The lighter the baggage, the easier the journey.
4. Selfishness will never be satisfying.
5. Indian spirituality transforms a person into a personality.
6. One should control the mind through vivek, the senses through the mind and go on to accept all of mankind as one united family.
7. Thinking of the self is kama, and only about the beloved is prema.
8. Make bhajan your nature.
9. After meeting God, one doesn't want to meet the world.
10. When life is disciplined, divine love comes naturally.
11. Give or take are the two streams of karma.
12. Seeking alms makes one humble.

16

Deva–Asura Sampad Vibhaga Yoga

The Yoga of Discerning the Divine and
Demonic Endowments

Total verses: 24

The last six chapters of Shrimad Bhagavad Gita elaborate on the intricacies of gyana, but the final three chapters explain its tenets in depth. They teach us the science of life and how to detach the soul from the physical body. To achieve this, we need to transcend the realm of the three gunas and surrender to Shree Purushottama. Once we perfect this devotion, nothing more is required. For me, karma, bhakti and gyana are one and the same, but being from the tradition, I am more inclined towards bhakti. Every karma should be done with utmost bhakti, that is, without any expectation whatsoever and with love for what we are doing. Each aspect of our life should be an extension of this triumvirate of karma, bhakti and gyana. This is the essence of Purushottama Yoga and becomes our orientation, our very nature. The light of the three gunas starts spreading before we realise Shree Purushottama. This illumination forms the foundation of this chapter, where the darkness of ignorance is dispelled. It details the progression of service, devotion and knowledge as we transcend the realm of the three gunas.

Shree Krishna vividly explains the swaroopa or the form of this universe, which is just an image of the Supreme. If the image is so beautiful, imagine how beautiful the creator and the original are. Every human is a fascinating combination of divine and demonic qualities. We all have the devil lurking within us, prodding us to pursue acts of self-destruction. When seen impartially, we understand that each individual has both good and evil tendencies. The percentage varies, but to say that there is no goodness at all in one who appears to be evil is wrong! Our success depends on how well we can utilise our positive qualities and marginalise the negativity within us. This chapter enumerates twenty-six divine traits and six general demonic tendencies. Shree Krishna reassures Arjuna that he is born divine. The scriptures say that in the Sat Yuga, the devas and the asuras lived on different planets. In the Treta Yuga, they lived on one planet as Rama and Ravana. In the Dvapara Yuga, they became a part of one family like the Kauravas and the Pandavas. As Kali Yuga came, they both reside within each of us. So, we all have the daevic and demonic tendencies within us. Mere existence is one thing, whereas to live is quite another.

In the Shrimad Bhagavatam, Shree Krishna, on the night of sharad purnima, plays His Divine flute.

Nishammyam geetam tadanagavardhanam, Vrajastriyaha
Krishnagraheetmaanasaha|
Aajagmuranyonyam lakshittodyamaha, sa yatra kanto java lok
kundalaha||

(The gopis of Vraja hearing the Divine melody of Shree Krishna's flute were mesmerised. Each one with their heart and soul immersed in the divine love of the lord ran towards Him, leaving everything behind) (Shrimad Bhagavatam 10:29:4).

This shloka says that we may be doing anything in life, but our focus should be the lord. In that case every action becomes His worship or service. We need to be conscious and alert to hear this divine music. Sadhus and mahatmas practise their spiritual austerities day in and day out, but for them it is neither repetitive nor boring. That's because their focus is attuned to the Divine, and they experience themselves getting closer to Him every moment. We can continually develop the sphere of our activity, beginning with the self and extending towards the welfare of mankind. In spirituality, the deeper we go, the more the same truths reveal newer meanings and our interest multiplies. We become what we think, so we must be mindful of our thoughts. We must practise reading our thoughts very carefully. The moment we start thinking positively, everything around us reflects that positivity—even in the most adverse circumstances. It is about placing things in the right perspective. Pain or happiness are part and parcel of life, and we must be alert in both the situations. Happiness instils humility, and pain teaches forbearance. As the outlook changes, everything changes without going anywhere. We are free to choose our karma. That is why we are the makers of our character and our own destiny.

The crucial difference between the divine and the demonic is knowledge. The divine have access to higher knowledge, whereas the demonic, deluded by greed, lust and ego, are ignorant of their true worth. Thus, they indulge in doing evil things. They do not know what to do or not to do, are impure and lack good conduct. They believe the world is meaningless and is brought about by delusion. Resorting to insatiable desire, and being of scant discrimination and savage deeds, such people destroy themselves and others. In the fourteen, fifteenth and sixteenth chapters, Arjuna has been a keen listener. Lord Krishna expounds on the different facets of human life, and guides Arjuna on how to find his way out of the maze that confuses mankind. In the first three verses of this chapter, Shree Krishna talks about the 'daevi' qualities.

Tejaha kshama dhritihi shauchamadroho naatimaanita|
Bhavanti sampaddam Daevim abhijatasya Bhaarata||
(Gita 16:3)

(Vigour, forgiveness, fortitude, purity, absence of hatred and the absence of pride belong to the one of Divine inclination, O Bharata.)

Nature, nurture and culture determine growth. Both Duryodhana and Arjuna are from the same gurukul, but their paths are opposite. Duryodhana has no qualms in admitting that he does not embody nobility. The farmers sow their seeds during a particular season, and this proves that the time and the situation of the seed's implantation are very important. Our scriptures explain this in great detail. An evil-minded person may disturb the environment of a noble family. At the same time, a pure soul may emerge that will purify a troubled household. Lord Krishna clarifies this point in the very first shloka of this chapter:

Abhayam satva sanshuddhiir gyana-yoga vyavasthitihi|
Daanam damashcha yagyashcha svaadhyayastapa aarjavam||
(Gita 16:1)

(Fearlessness, purity of heart, steadfastness in knowledge or Gyana Yoga, charity, control of the senses, sacrifice, study of the scriptures and straightforwardness.)

We need to delve within and honestly examine how many qualities we possess. The list of daevi traits, as explained by Lord Krishna, include: fearlessness, purification of existence, cultivation of spiritual knowledge, charity, self-control, sacrifice, self-study, austerity, simplicity, non-violence, truthfulness, freedom from anger, being free of ego or pride, tranquillity, not faulting others, compassion, non-covetousness, gentle, modest, firm determination, vigour, forgiving, fortitude, cleanliness, non-envy and non-expectant of honour. In contrast, demonic traits are hypocrisy, arrogance, deceit, pride, anger, harshness and ignorance. While we can elaborate on each of these, I feel that most of us already have an intuitive understanding of them. Going into the intricacies will become very exhaustive.

Dambho darpo abhimanashcha kridhaha paarushyameva cha|
Agyanam chaabhijaatasya Partha sampadamaasurim||
(Gita 16:4)

(Hypocrisy, arrogance and self-conceit, anger, harshness and ignorance belong to the one born of the demonic tendency, O Partha.)

Daevi sampadvimokshaya nibandhayasuri mutta|
'Ma shuchaha' sampadam Daevim abhijatoasi Pandava||
(Gita 16:5)

(The divine nature is deemed for liberation, the demonical for bondage; do not grieve nor doubt, O 'Pandava', you are born with divine qualities.)

Shree Krishna uses *'Ma shuchaha'* twice in the Gita. Once here, and again in the sixty-sixth verse of the eighteenth chapter. Here, it refers to the means or the sadhan, and there, it is in the context of siddhi or perfection. The lord assures His dear devotee that he should have no apprehension about performing truthful actions, nor about his liberation. For ease of understanding, Lord Krishna has explained both traits in detail.

The seed is a thought. We experience an emptiness within, and then thoughts arise in the mind, eventually going into the world to acquire objects and associate with others. One mistakenly feels that this will fill the void, resulting in the indulgence of sensory pleasures. One leads to another and lands up in a moha jala, a web of delusion. People are addicted to sensory gratification, causing their downfall. Then, one leads a stressful life devoid of vitality, joy and growth. Pleasure becomes pain, and life is a nightmare. The self-conceited, obstinate and arrogant perform sacrifices ostentatiously, against scriptural mandate. Ignorant of one's divinity, people enter this endless cycle of birth and death, taking birth in a demonic environment. Not realising the truth, without correcting oneself, people go on slipping into lower life forms. People thus deluded and mired by evil say:

Asatyampratishtham tey jagadahurneeshwaram|
Aparaspara sambhootam kimanyatkamahaitukam||
(Gita 16:8)

(They say that the universe is without truth and any basis for God. It is not brought about by any regular causal sequence but with lust as the cause of its birth.)

Ettamdrishttim vashtabhya nashtatmano alpabuddhayaha|
Prabhavantyugra karmanaha kshayaya jagatohitaha||
(Gita 16:9)

(With this view, these ruined souls of small intellect and evil deeds come forth as the enemies of mankind, pursuing its destruction.)

We must pay attention to these four things in life: wishes, desires, conduct, tradition, and correctness or suitability. They form our dos and don'ts. Lord Krishna clarifies this in the eighteenth verse, '*Ahankaram balam darpam kamam krodham cha sanshritaha* (Given to egoism, power, haughtiness, lust and anger, these people hate me).' Till now, Lord Krishna has explained the demonic traits in detail. In the last two verses, He says:

Yaha shastravidhimutsrajya varatattey kamakaarataha|
Na sa sidhimavapnoti na sukham na parram gattim||
(Gita 16:23)

(One who has cast aside the ordinance of the scriptures acts under the impulse of desire, attains neither perfection, nor happiness, nor the ultimate goal.)

Tasmaachha shastram pramanam ttey kaaryakarya vyavasthittau
Gyattva shastravidhanoktam karma kartum ehaarhasi||
(Gita 16:24)

(So, let the scriptures be your guide in determining what should be done and what should not. Having known what is said in the commandments of the scriptures, you should act accordingly.)

I have intentionally not delved into the evils as explained by Lord Krishna, because I believe that whether others know or not, we certainly know ourselves. Our basic nature is godly: '*Eashwara ansa jeeva avinasi* (Jeeva is a tiny part of ishwara or the Almighty)' (Ramcharitmanas). However, maya deludes us into believing what we are not, and we are sucked into the black hole of evil. Let me emphasise that everything in the scriptures is scientific and practical. In our temples, certain procedures are laid down, like the type of clothing to wear, the utensils used for puja, the methodology to be followed, etc. After describing the perils of yielding to devilish tendencies, Shree Krishna urges us to free ourselves from the three gates of hell—desire, anger and greed. Anger and greed are the mutations of desire. Therefore, we need to overcome desire. Yet, today, we encourage, fan and promote desire. People don't understand its devastating effect. The doors of our soul are shut, preventing us from realising our power and magnificence. If we follow our divine nature, we not only do good to ourselves but also uplift others. We lead a successful and a happy life, eventually transcending the world, attaining moksha.

We often take the easy way out and give in to negative tendencies. Sadly, the best within us lies dormant, unknown, untapped and unacknowledged. The Gita shows us the way out of this dungeon of ignorance into the light of wisdom.

SUMMARY

Verses 1–9: The description of the divine and demonic traits.
Verses 10–18: The description of demonic actions.
Verses 19–22: The result of doing evil.
Verses 23–24: In conclusion, Lord Krishna shows the way.

KEY QUOTES

1. Until one doesn't know the reality, he believes the illusion to be real.
2. You are what you think.
3. Before doing anything, think about the purpose behind it.
4. Studying the scriptures and worshipping God are divine actions.
5. Before explaining anything, one needs to understand it.
6. Don't tell the Almighty about the magnitude of your problems; instead, tell the problem how mighty God is!
7. One who is filled with abuse and arrogance will speak harshly.
8. Accept respect with humility, but don't expect it.
9. You are the creator of your character, life and destiny.
10. When our thinking changes, our outlook changes automatically.
11. One should use the power of one's thought to excel in life, not to destroy it.
12. One who has divinity will be fearless.
13. Laugh, but please don't laugh at someone.
14. A child learns more by observing than by learning.
15. A Vedic way of life uplifts!
16. Keep on observing your thoughts, or else you will get negatively influenced.

17

Shraddha Traya Vibhaga Yoga

The Yoga of the Division of Threefold Faith

Total verses: 28

In the sixteenth chapter, Shree Krishna says that a person who just pursues desires while ignoring the directions of the scriptures attains neither success nor happiness. He will not make any spiritual progress. This chapter addresses a very important topic: shraddha (faith). In the beginning, Goswami Tulsidas Ji states, '*Bhawani Shankarau vanddey Shraddha Vishwas roopinau* (I bow down to Ma Bhawani and Lord Shankara, who are the embodiment of faith and trust)' (Ramcharitmanas 1:2). Nothing exists without faith and trust. The concept of threefold faith explores the nature of shraddha and its influence on our nature and character. Here, faith forms the bedrock of spirituality. However, faith, as often translated, is not the exact meaning of shraddha; it has a far deeper connotation. It is a synthesis of devotion and intellectual focus that is maintained with clarity until a goal is achieved. It is the ability to envision a goal and consistently strive towards it. Shraddha is the most important determinant of success. It defines us. One may be exceptionally talented, well-educated and have all the opportunities. But unless one consistently applies them wholeheartedly, the goal will remain elusive. Our scriptures declare, '*Aaddau Shraddha*', that is, shraddha is foremost. Being dharmic while fulfilling our responsibilities is not complicated. Our nature expresses our faith, which affects our actions. In this chapter, Lord Krishna explains the three types of shraddha, corresponding to the three modes of material nature: sattva, rajas and tamas.

The environment around us is filled with negativity. There is positivity within us, but the predominance of negative tendencies ensures it remains latent. Shraddha is an aspect of one's nature or vasana. Our sages analysed the human mind and explored its very root. Thus, their prescription for inner development is scientific and rational. There are no grey areas here. Arjuna understands this problem, and in the very first verse, he questions Lord Krishna as to what the fate is of one who disregards the mandate of the scriptures. Yet, if such a person performs yagna, what is his fate?

The reason behind naming this chapter 'Shraddha Traya Vibhaga Yoga' is revealed in the third shloka. Shree Krishna, who says that we become what we believe in, speaks of three types of shraddha. Sattvic shraddha is the worship of gods, the divine manifestations and higher ideals. Rajasic is the worship of gods as ends in themselves or the pursuit of material, self-centred goals. Tamasic people are oblivious of the transcendental and lead a lazy, lackadaisical life of ignorance. They worship ghosts and spirits. They are unwilling to work and resort to bizarre means, hoping to achieve success.

Prakriti is trigunamayi, that is, an amalgam of the three. Tamas is like a wrapper or a covering. The rajasic is vikshep (perplexity), and sattvic is divine knowledge. The characteristics of each of these are as follows:

Sattvic: Knowledge, purity, divinity, welfare of others, effortless, early riser, detachment, active in divine actions, subtle intellect, endearing to all, far-sighted, indifferent, humble, devoted towards saints and acharyas, and will work with gay abandon.

Rajasic: Perplexed, moody, works objectively, harmful, show-off, wastes time, obsessive, busy doing nothing, materialistic, selfish, seeks instant gratification, does only what interests him, arrogant, appeasing the powers that be and will go to any extent for self-gain.

Tamasic: Mental blindness, shrouded in darkness, voluptuous, self-destructive, lazy, night owl, self-obsessed, inactive, ignorant, braggart, egoist, disgusting and fears being punished as well as death.

This chapter has twenty-eight verses. From verses 1 to 7, Shree Krishna explains worship and the different forms of shraddha. This is then further divided into food, yajna, charity and austerity. '*Om tat sat*' is the symbolic representation of the Supreme Absolute Truth. Om indicates the Supreme: pranava. Tat is for unshackling from material bondage. Sat is the Absolute Truth, the sole object of all worship. Any sacrifice or austerities performed without faith are termed 'asat' or impermanent.

Trividha bhavati shraddha dehinaam sa svabhaavaja|
Satviki rajasi chaiva, tamasi cheti ttam shrunu||
(Gita 17:2)

Satvanuroopa sarvasya shraddha bhavati Bhaarata|
Shraddhamayoayam purusho yo yachhraddhaha sa eva saha||
(Gita 17:3)

(Threefold is the faith of the embodied, which is inherent; sattvic, rajasic and tamasic. The faith of each is by their nature. One is made up according to one's faith; as the faith, so is he!)

The pious worship the divine, the rajasic worship the demons, and the tamasic worship ghosts and spirits.

Aaharastvapi sarvasys trividho bhavati priyaha|
Yagyastapastatha daanam teysham bhedmimam shrinu||
(Gita 17:7)

(People prefer according to their dispositions. The same is true for yagna, austerity and charity, which are based on their predisposition. Now, I explain their distinctions.)

Shree Krishna now goes on to describe the classification of ahara (food), yagna (sacrifice), tapas (austerity) and dana (charity). They are classified into sattvic, rajasic and tamasic. The analysis of these into the three gunas helps to get an idea of one's inner nature. Every aspect of a person's personality is coloured with a particular combination of the gunas.

Food has a direct connection with our minds. Sattvic food is tasty, wholesome, nutritious, and assures longevity of life, vigour, good health and happiness. The common misconception is that one becomes spiritual if one consumes sattvic food. But it is only partially true. Food plays an important role in moulding one's disposition. These days, an organic, vegan, nutritional and wholesome diet has gained popularity. The fasting that is practised in different religions aids self-control. Even intermittent fasting has become a craze. Rajasic people like pungent, spicy and a wide variety of dishes. At times, when eaten in excess, it causes discomfort, and one gets sick. Stale, tasteless, putrid, polluted, and leftovers are the natural choice of those who are tamasic. Dieticians also prescribe that one should eat 50 per cent of one's hunger, 25 per cent should be consumption of water and keep the balance empty to be healthy.

From verses 11 to 13, the different types of yagna are explained. A sattvic yagna is performed without any desire or personal gain. It is a sacrifice performed as duty, with a peaceful mind, and according to scriptural guidance and wisdom. A rajasic yagna is done for personal gain. The yagna performed overlooking the scriptures, without offering any food to the needy, with an ulterior motive or for harming someone is a tamasic yagna.

From verses 14 to 19, Lord Krishna explains the different types of tapas: physical, verbal and mental. This threefold austerity performed steadfastly with shraddha, without any desire whatsoever, is sattvic. The rajasic tapas is temporary, unstable and motivated by selfish wants such as gaining respect or name and fame. The misguided, self-tormenting practices done with deluded obstinacy and to harm others are tamasic. Shree Krishna in the Vibhuti Yoga declared, 'Yagyanam Japaha yagyosmi (Amongst all the sacrifices, I am Japa Yagna).' Repeating, chanting or singing the Divine name is indeed the greatest, especially during this age of Kali. Shree Chaitanya Mahaprabhu propagated and established the naam japa, and today, it has become a worldwide movement.

Manaha prasadaha saumyattvam maunamatmnigraha|
Bhavasanshuddhirityeta tapo manasuchhyattey||
(Gita 17:16)

(Serenity of thought, gentleness, silence or maun, self-control and purity of purpose are all the austerities of the mind.)

Threefold austerity (thought, word and deed) is practised by the yogis with supreme faith and is said to be in the mode of goodness. This tapa results in contentment and serenity. To continuously examine the thoughts that arise in the mind and to exercise control is known as manasi tapa, or the austerity of the mind.

From verses 20 to 22, Shree Krishna talks about dana. We are constantly presented opportunities to give, but we must do so from the heart, not just with the hand. Acts of charity have immense benefits for the donor and the recipient. A gift given without any expectation of a reward in return to a worthy person at the right time and the right place is sattvic dana. Anything given grudgingly to gain something in return is rajasic, and a gift given contemptuously to an unworthy person at an inappropriate time and place is tamasic. Now, from verses 23 to 28, Lord Krishna gives His conclusion.

> *Om tat satditi nirdesho brahmanstrividhaha smritaha|*
> *Braahmanastena Vedashcha yagyashcha vihitaha pura||*
> (Gita 17:23)

(The words 'Om Tat Sat' have been declared as the symbolic representation of the Supreme Absolute Truth since eternity. From it emanated the Brahman, the scriptures and yagna.)

In the eighth chapter, Lord Krishna says, '*Pranava sarva Vedeshu* (I am the Pranava in the Vedas).' In the Brahma Sutras it says, '*Tat tu samanvayaat* (Tat means that "one" Brahman).' The Vedantin says, 'You are that.' But the followers of the Bhakti tradition say, 'You become His or you love Him.' 'Om' is the most important word in Sanatana; in Islam, it is 'ameen'; in Christianity, it is 'amen'. Ultimately, it is the same. 'Sat' is the ultimate truth. Therefore, Brahman or the Supreme is indicated by Om Tat Sat. This is the path to the ultimate reality. 'Om' is the subtlest symbol of the Supreme and the most powerful mantra for meditation. 'Tat' is 'that', the supreme state of enlightenment. 'Sat' is goodness, the ultimate truth and remaining steadfast in the pursuit of yagna, tapa and dana. When these three are performed without faith or shraddha, it becomes 'asat'.

This chapter offers profound insights into the connection between faith, actions and personal growth. By understanding the influence of the three gunas, we gain valuable tools for self-reflection and transformation. This awareness brings a conscious shift towards noble qualities, which nurture harmony, spiritual upliftment and inner peace. Faith, as described in this chapter, is the dynamic force that shapes character and destiny. By integrating sattvic principles through mindful worship, a balanced lifestyle and selfless actions, one can align with higher spiritual values and contribute positively to the world.

These teachings encourage us to view life as an opportunity for growth and service. Faith becomes an active force, enabling us to rise above ignorance and selfish desires, while embracing clarity, compassion and purpose. Cultivating a sattvic way of life ensures a deeper connection with the Divine and brings fulfilment through the adherence to dharma. This chapter reminds us that true transformation starts within. It urges us to live with balance, integrity and a lasting sense of peace. Service and sadhana are not separate. Our karma should be performed with a sense of service, which then becomes a service to God. When we inculcate yagna, dana and tapa in our life, there will be no frictions in society. The community becomes more accommodating. This will generate peace and harmony all around.

SUMMARY

Verses 1–7:   The three types of shraddha.
Verses 8–10:   The types of food.
Verses 11–13: The types of yagna.
Verses 14–19: The types of tapas.
Verses 20–22: The types of dana.
Verses 23–28: Description of Om Tat Sat.

QUOTES

1. The Gita reveals to us what lies within.
2. The Gita offers a cure, not just a remedy.
3. The Gita equips us to create noble traits.
4. Control your thoughts and purify them.
5. When food is pure, the mind will be too.

18

Moksha Sanyas Yoga

Liberation Through Renunciation

Total verses: 79

We have now reached the eighteenth chapter of the Gita. In my opinion, it might be the conclusion of this great text, but in reality, it is now that Arjuna, the devotee, unconditionally surrendering at the Lotus Feet of the Supreme Lord, says, *'Karishye vachanam tava* (I will follow whatever you instruct)' (Gita 18:73). This divine text is eternal: *'Hari anant Hari katha ananta* (Hari is infinite and so is His katha).' Each person has the liberty to interpret it as per his or her understanding. There are hundreds of commentaries available, and we are at liberty to write our own. In English, we say water; in Hindi, it is jal; in Urdu, paani; in Arabic, maa; in Mandarin, shuǐ; in French, eau; in German, das Wasser; in Hebrew, mayim—and so on. It has different names, but water's basic characteristics as the source of our seas, rivers, lakes and rain remain the same. Similarly, the Supreme Personality of Godhead is the same entity, having many different names. The Ultimate Reality is *one*. This chapter deals with liberation through renunciation. John Milton wrote his epic poem, *Paradise Lost*, in 1667. He explored themes of disobedience, redemption, and the nature of good and evil, all a part of human nature. This eternal text was narrated more than 5,000 years ago and talks about the different facets of human life, much before Western thinkers contemplated them. When we refer to the lord, it signifies the Supreme Reality, and is the same.

Man can create both heaven and hell on Earth; while we marvel at the beauty created by God, we also witness the exploitation and degradation caused by man. When we consider the background of the Bhagavad Gita, we realise that it is a dialogue in the middle of a battlefield, and both armies are arrayed to fight. Amid all this chaos, Shree Krishna recreates paradise for Arjuna, and through him, teaches us the way to lead a meaningful life. Or if I may say, granting us the key to paradise! Bhagwan Kapil in his *Sankhya Yoga* says, '*Atraiva narakaha swarga iti mataha prachakshattey* (Hell and heaven both exist here)' (Srimad Bhagavatam 3:30:29). There are three situations, first where there is pleasure but no peace. Second, where there is peace and no desire for pleasure, and the third, where there is both peace and pleasure.

Shree Krishna says, '*Na maam karmaani limpanti na mey karma phaley spriha* (The karma doesn't bind me nor do I have any expectation of any fruits of my actions)' (Gita 4:14). The premise of this chapter is based on liberation and renunciation. In reality, man is free, but he sees himself to be fettered and bound. This chapter clarifies our true nature, which is free, and then explains the true meaning of renunciation. It is, in a way, the summary of the entire Gita. With seventy-eight verses, it is the longest chapter. Every verse has profound significance, but I will focus on the most salient ones. Here, Lord Krishna clearly differentiates between sanyas and tyag, that is, renunciation and relinquishing or resignation. Renunciation means letting go of action motivated by desire. Relinquishing means giving up the fruits of action. Contrary to popular conception, Lord Krishna emphasised that although embodied beings cannot completely relinquish action, they must relinquish the results of action. Verses 49 and 50 talk about mystical knowledge. Verses 61 to 63 talk about divine knowledge, and verses 64 to 66 talk of the supreme knowledge. This knowledge is highly confidential.

Sanyasasya Mahabaho tattvamichhami veditum|
Tyagasya cha Hrishikesha prithakayshinishudana||
(Gita 18:1)

(Arjuna asks the Lord, I wish to understand the nature of sanyasa and tyag. O Hrishikesha! I also wish to know the distinction between the two, O Keshinisudana!)

Neither sanyas nor tyag implies abandoning action. We must act, but we must give up two things that hinder excellence of action: desires from the past, and anxiety for the fruit that belongs to the future. Yes, desire is necessary to initiate the action. Similarly, there is always a desired fruit of the action in our mind before we act. However, while executing an action, 100 per cent of the mind must be focused solely on what we are doing. If the mind meanders into the dead past or the unborn future, it is not concentrating on the present. Such action becomes faulty and ineffective, eventually leading to failure. In the first six chapters, Shree Krishna asks us to act without craving for a desired outcome. In the first twelve verses, He explains this very point in detail so that it gets ingrained in our psyche.

Lord Krishna explains how some sages say that all action should be renounced as flawed, while others maintain that yagna, tapa and dana should never be abandoned. The vast majority of people are laden with desire. They need to perform acts of sacrifice, charity and austerity to purify themselves. For them, action is sans attachment, and the fruit is the pathway to spiritual evolution. The rare one—on the verge of realisation and completely absorbed in meditation—must let go of even the last thought, which is now the impediment. It prevents him from taking off into an exalted state of enlightenment. He needs to give up all actions and vasanas, the last one being the desire of realisation.

Five elements are present whenever an action takes place: the physical body, the agent, the sensory organs, behaviour and the Divine. Those with limited understanding see themselves as the sole agent of an action and fail to recognise these five components. Shree Krishna divides the three concepts of knowledge, action and agent into their respective gunas. These three, along with intellect, fortitude and joy, are each categorised as sattvic, rajasic and tamasic. This conclusively proves that no one or anything is free from the three gunas. We are neither the doer nor the controller. Lord Krishna tells Arjuna, 'Nimittamatram bhava Savyasachin (Become the instrument)' (Gita 11:33). Detach yourself from the sense of doership as well as the controller of the result or fruit of your action. From verses 19 to 40, Lord Krishna explains the distinction between the action, the sensory organs, the physical body, the doer and the paramatman.

Sattvic knowledge comprehends that all beings are 'undivided among the divided'; they are truly one single unchanging being. The notion of being separate is relinquished. Knowledge that perceives the world as a place of separate and disconnected individual beings is rajasic. Tamasic knowledge doesn't care about the truth. Action is sattvic when it has pure motives, whereas rajasic action is done to satisfy desires. However, He warns that even the most noble acts should be done with complete detachment. Tamasic action stems from delusion and complete disdain. The concepts of understanding, will and happiness are each characterised by the three gunas. Lord Krishna describes happiness in terms of poison and nectar. For those with rajasic tendencies, seeking happiness through sensory pleasures or greed turns nectar into poison.

For those who practise austerities, the effort is rigorous; it seems like poison but becomes nectar. For those driven by delusion or ignorance, it is always poison.

Verses 41 to 48 address the karma done without any desire. Lord Krishna explains the Varnashrama dharma. Based on one's inner composition, all humans are categorised into four varnas (castes). This distinction isn't based on lineage but on the proportion of sattva, rajas and tamas within an individual. A mismatch of inner composition with the external work can be frustrating and prevent progress. Transgressing this distinction, Shree Chaitanya Mahaprabhu said, '*Naaham vipronacha narapati naiva Vaishya na shoodro, nova varno na cha grihapati mo vanasthothatirva| Kintu prodyana Nikhil Paramanand Poornamamritabdhey, Gopi bharturpadakamaleyyo dasdaasanudasa* (Mahaprabhu merely states that I belong to no caste at all. I am the servant of the servant of the servant of the Lotus Feet of Shree Krishna, the beloved of the gopis. He is the ocean of nectar and the cause of the universal transcendental bliss who glows with brilliance).'

By engaging in our duties and offering our actions to the Divine, we purify our mind of all selfishness and reach a state of *gyana nishta yogyata*—the qualification for devotion to knowledge. When seekers reach this stage, they engage in the life of a sanyasi, enabling them to contemplate upon the nature of the atman and the self, and remain devoted to the Divine, the final stage of the spiritual journey. From the verses 49 to 55, Shree Krishna explains that performing karma without any expectation (Nishkama Karma) leads to the attainment of knowledge and moksha. From verses 46 to 57, Lord Krishna captures the complete spiritual path. He starts with the three practices of Karma Yoga, Bhakti Yoga and Gyana Yoga, and ends with meditation. He cautions Arjuna and through him all of us, on the consequences of disregarding His advice. If we shift our focus to the atman, we will overcome all such obstacles. If we ignore the divinity and lose ourselves in the material realms, we shall perish! Even the most perfect yogis find bhakti to be the highest, most transcendental realisation of Brahman. Thus, only through loving devotion can one unravel the secrets of the Supreme Divine Personality. Finally, He reminds Arjuna that God dwells in the hearts of all living creatures and directs their movement according to their karmas. From verses 56 to 60, Shree Krishna enlightens as well as motivates His devotee. He prods us to strive on the path of bhakti without losing heart after which we shall reach our goal. From verses 61 to 63, He talks of complete surrender. Seeking Him, we must surrender unto Him, take His refuge and offer all our actions at His Lotus Feet. This way, we can transcend the entrappings of maya. Through His grace, we will make progress in our spiritual journey. The sixty-fourth shloka is very mysterious:

> *Sarva guhyattamam bhooyaha shrinu mey paramam vachaha|*
> *Ishtosi mey dridhamiti tattoo vakshyami tey hitam||*
> (Gita 18:64)

(Hear again my supreme instruction, which is most confidential of all knowledge. I am revealing this just for your benefit because you are very dear to me.)

> *Manmana bhava maddbhakto maddyaji maam namaskuru|*
> *Maamaivaishyasi satyam tey pratijaney priyosi mey||*
> (Gita 18:65)

(Always think of me, be devoted to me, worship me and offer obeisance to me. By doing so, you will certainly come to me. This is my promise to you, for you are very dear to me.)

Shree Krishna reveals the innermost secrets to Arjuna, for he is His devotee and very dear to Him. In His own words, He says, '*Aham bhakta paraadheeno* (I am subservient to my devotee).' Now, He comes out with the most reassuring of all statements, saying:

Sarvadharman parityajya maamekam sharanam vraja|
Aham tvam sarva paapebhyo mokshaishyami ma shuchaha||
(Gita 18:66)

(Abandon all the dharmas and simply surrender unto me! I promise that I shall absolve you from all the sinful reactions, have no doubt about it.)

My sadguru used to say, 'Khuda bada hota hai, banda chhota hota hai, per jab ishq ki hadi ho jaati hai toh Khuda bhi bandey kay neechey aa jata hai (God is big and the devotee is very small but when the ishq [divine love] reaches its peak the devotee becomes bigger than God).' From verses 67 to 71, Lord Krishna lays down the criteria of who is an able recipient of this divine knowledge.

Iddam tey naatapaskaaya na bhaktaaya kadachana|
Na chashushrushavey vaachyam na cha maam yo abhyasooyati||
(Gita 18:67)

(This knowledge should never be explained to those who are not austere or to those who are not devoted. It should not be given to those who are averse to listening to the spiritual texts, and especially not to those who envy me.)

Ya iddam paramam guhyyam maddbhakteyshva abhidhasyati|
Bhaktim mayi paraam kritva maameyvaishyatya sanshayaha||
(Gita 18:68)

(Amongst my devotees, those who teach this most confidential knowledge perform the greatest service. They will doubtlessly come to me.)

Na cha tasmanmanushyeshu kashchinnmey priyakrittamaha|
Bhavita na cha may tasmaad anyaha priyataro bhuvi||
(Gita 18:69)

(No one serves me more than these, nor shall there ever be anyone dearer to me.)

Shraddhavaanan sooyashcha shrinuyadapi yo Naraha|
Soapi muktaha shubhaanlokkan praapnuyaat punyakarannam||
(Gita 18:71)

(Those who listen to this knowledge with faith and without envy will be liberated from all sins and attain auspicious abodes of the pious.)

Kachhitdetuchhuttam Partha tvayaikaagrena chetasa|
Kachhidgyan sammohaha pranashtatey Dhananjaya||
(Gita 18:72)

(Hey Arjuna! Have you concentrated on my sermon? Now, has your illusion and ignorance been destroyed?)

Out of His sheer benevolence, Lord Krishna narrates the entire divine knowledge to Arjuna. Then, he asks if he requires further explanations. To me, the most important shloka is when Arjuna completely surrenders at the Lotus Feet of the Lord and says that he will do as He commands:

Nashto mohaha smritirlabhdha tvatprasadaan mayachyuta|
Sthitosmi gatasandehaha karshyey vachannam tava||
(Gita 18:73)

(Arjuna says, 'My Lord! By your divine grace, my illusion has been dispelled and I am now firm in my understanding. I am now free from doubts and I shall do whatever you instruct'.)

My sadguru would say, 'Smar+rana+marana, smar=kama, rana=war and marana=death. Whatever liberates you from this is smarana.' The Gita's greatest blessing is the constant remembrance of Shree Krishna. Finally, Lord Krishna leaves us to do as we wish. The Bhagavad Gita is not a doctrine of instructions or commandments.

It is a manual of guidance, a logical, scientific treatise on the human personality. We need to reflect on these principles, examine them from all angles, experiment with them and then draw our conclusions. Once we do this exercise, only then we can live by them, experience the truths laid down in the Gita and find liberation in the world. We can live like a king, think like a sanyasi, commanding the resources of the world without depending on them. In the beginning of the first chapter, Dhritarashtra asks Sanjaya about the war at Kurukshetra. In verses 74 to 78, he is narrating his analysis of all that he has witnessed. He concludes:

Yatra Yogeshwaraha Krishno yatra Partho dhanurdharaha|
Tatra Shreervijayo bhutidhrova nettirmatirmuma||
(Gita 18:78)

(Wherever there is Yogeshwar Shree Krishna and wherever there is the supreme archer Arjuna, most certainly there will be unending opulence, victory, prosperity and righteousness. I am sure of it.)

Om Tat Sat iti Shrimad Bhagavad Gitasu Upanishadsu Bramhavidyayam yogashastry Shree Krishna Arjuna samvadey Moksha Sanyas Yogo naam ashtadasho adhyayaha Shree Radha Raman Charan Kamal arpanmastu||

While this is the conclusion of our discussion on the Gita, factually, it is a new dawn in our lives. These eighteen chapters were narrated over eighteen days when we were all locked down due to the raging pandemic. During those days, time was not a constraint, and by the benevolence of my sadguru and the Shrimad Bhagavad Gita Mata, certain thoughts came to my mind. I thought it was the right time to devote to studying and meditating on this divine text. I have undoubtedly immensely benefited from this, and I am confident that it shall be a valuable reference for all of us. While deeply rooted in the Hindu philosophy, the Bhagavad Gita transcends religious boundaries. Its teachings resonate with seekers from all backgrounds, offering universal wisdom that applies to the human experience as a whole. Its relevance is eternal because it emphasises ethical behaviour, selflessness and mindfulness, providing a map to navigate contemporary challenges. The core of the Gita is not about renouncing the world but rather living in alignment with the divine purpose, and free from the shackles of attachment and ego. It is a guide to understanding the true nature of the Ultimate Reality. Like the Supreme is eternal and infinite, so are His words. The Gita is the foundation of a meaningful and a purposeful life. Its teachings provide solace, guidance and enlightenment, making it a timeless spiritual companion for humanity as a whole. This reflection is just a drop in that vast ocean of divine knowledge. The entire knowledge of the cosmos is contained in these 700 verses of the Gita. It forms the essence of the four Vedas, 108 Upanishads and the six systems of Hindu philosophy.

My prayers at the Divine Lotus Feet of Shree Radha Raman Dev Ji to bless us all with loving devotion and may we all become 'human' in the right sense.

SUMMARY

Verses 1–12:   Talk about karma
Verses 13–18: Talk about gyana.
Verses 19–40: The three types of karma.
Verses 41–48: Karma with and without desire.
Verses 49–55: The attainment of knowledge through Nishkama Karma, leading to moksha with the stress on bhakti.
Verses 56–60: The nature of bhakti and sewa.
Verses 61–63: Surrendering to the Almighty.
Verses 64–66: Complete surrender unto Shree Krishna.
Verses 67–71: Studying, teaching and propagating the teachings of the Gita.

Verses 72–73: Arjuna's total surrender.
Verses 74–78: Sanjaya's conclusion.

KEY QUOTES

1. The Bhagavad Gita helps to create heaven within us.
2. We can understand liberation only when we know what is bondage.
3. Through the body, the mind and understanding, take the consciousness towards the atman.
4. The physical body, the mind and the intellect are prisons, while the atman is ever free.
5. We need to move from partisanship to being neutral.
6. Remove the notion of doership from whatever you are doing, this is gyana.
7. By hearing or studying the Gita, we don't become God, but we become His.
8. Leave everything, surrender totally and unconditionally unto Him, and He will do everything!